P9-BIU-167

DEFINED

Who God Says You Are

LifeWay Press®
Nashville, Tennessee

Editorial Team

Jeremy Maxfield
Writer

Reid Patton
Content Editor

David Haney
Production Editor

Jon Rodda
Art Director

Joel Polk
Editorial Team Leader

Brian Daniel
Manager, Short-Term Discipleship

Michael Kelley
Director, Discipleship and Groups Ministry

Published by LifeWay Press® • © 2019 Kendrick Bros., LLC
Used under License. All Rights Reserved.

Movie images and photography (pp. 8–9): AFFIRM Films A Sony Company
© 2019 Columbia TriStar Marketing Group, Inc. All Rights Reserved.

No part of this book may be reproduced or transmitted in any form or by any means, electronic or mechanical, including photocopying and recording, or by any information storage or retrieval system, except as may be expressly permitted in writing by the publisher. Requests for permission should be addressed in writing to LifeWay Press®; One LifeWay Plaza; Nashville, TN 37234.

ISBN 978-1-4627-9496-6 • Item 005802010

Dewey decimal classification: 248.84
Subject headings: SELF-REALIZATION / CHRISTIAN LIFE /
IDENTITY (PSYCHOLOGY)

Unless indicated otherwise, Scripture quotations are taken from the Christian Standard Bible®, Copyright © 2017 by Holman Bible Publishers. Used by permission. Christian Standard Bible® and CSB® are federally registered trademarks of Holman Bible Publishers. Scripture quotations marked NASB are taken from the New American Standard Bible® (NASB), Copyright © 1960, 1962, 1963, 1968, 1971, 1972, 1973, 1975, 1977, 1995 by The Lockman Foundation. Used by permission. www.lockman.org. Scripture quotations marked NLT are taken from the Holy Bible, New Living Translation, copyright ©1996, 2004, 2007, 2013, 2015 by Tyndale House Foundation. Used by permission of Tyndale House Publishers, Inc., Carol Stream, IL 60188. All rights reserved.

To order additional copies of this resource, write to LifeWay Resources Customer Service; One LifeWay Plaza; Nashville, TN 37234; fax 615-251-5933; call toll free 800-458-2772; order online at LifeWay.com; or email orderentry@lifeway.com.

Printed in the United States of America

Groups Ministry Publishing • LifeWay Resources • One LifeWay Plaza • Nashville, TN 37234

Contents

About the Authors

STEPHEN KENDRICK is a speaker, a film producer, and an author with a ministry passion for prayer and discipleship. He's a cowriter and the producer of the movies *OVERCOMER, WAR ROOM,* and *FIREPROOF* and a cowriter of the *New York Times* best sellers *The Resolution for Men* and *The Love Dare.* An ordained minister, Stephen attended seminary, received a communications degree from Kennesaw State University, and serves on the board of the Fatherhood CoMission. Stephen and his family live in Albany, Georgia, where they're members of Sherwood Church. Most important, as affirmed by this Bible study, he's a child of God whose citizenship is in heaven.

ALEX KENDRICK is an award-winning author gifted at telling stories of hope and redemption. He's best known as an actor, a cowriter, and the director of the films *FIREPROOF, COURAGEOUS, FACING THE GIANTS, WAR ROOM,* and *OVERCOMER* and a coauthor of the *New York Times* best-selling books *The Love Dare, The Resolution for Men, Fireproof* (novel), and *Courageous* (novel). In 2002 Alex helped found Sherwood Pictures and partnered with his brother, Stephen, to launch Kendrick Brothers Productions. He's a graduate of Kennesaw State University and attended seminary before being ordained to ministry. Alex and his family live in Albany, Georgia, where they're members of Sherwood Church.

JEREMY MAXFIELD, who developed the Bible study, lives in Chattanooga, Tennessee, with his wife, their three daughters, and a chocolate lab. After earning degrees from the University of Georgia and Beeson Divinity School, he has served in various pastoral roles over the past fifteen years and in Christian publishing for ten years. You can find more of his work at jeremymaxfield.com and can follow him on Twitter @jrmaxfield.

Introduction

Who is God?

Who am I?

Perhaps you mostly already know the answers to these two questions, you'd say. You know who God is, basically. You know who you are, basically. Or perhaps you'd say nobody can really know these answers, not enough to get past all their philosophical aspects where they can do a person any practical good.

But actually, these two basic questions and their answers are of immense, gut-level importance to the everyday life you're experiencing right now. Even in their simplicity these questions speak to your complexity. They're not just philosophical. They're essential. They're imperative. They're tied directly and distinctly to your right-this-moment concerns and problems.

And even if you indeed know solid answers to each of them, human beings are always subject to believing lies or distortions about them and then ingesting those lies as truth, based on the unreliable gauges of feelings, opinions, or cultural pressure.

Good news: the truth we all need in seeking answers to these vital questions has been made abundantly available to us. In the Bible. God Himself has told us.

The next piece of good news, though it's somewhat unexpected, is that these two questions are permanently joined together. The more we know and understand God—Who is God?—the better we can know and understand ourselves—Who am I? We can answer both answers at the same time. And that's what this Bible study is about.

The Creator defines His creation, and because God created you, discovering who He is will tell you who you are. Over the next eight weeks you'll seek to learn about God and yourself and to apply the answers to these questions in your life.

How to Use This Study

This Bible-study book includes eight weeks of content for group and personal study.

Group Sessions

Regardless of what day of the week your group meets, each week of content begins with the group session. Each group session uses the following format to facilitate simple yet meaningful interaction among group members, with God's Word, and with the teaching of Stephen and Alex Kendrick.

START. This page includes questions to get the conversation started and to introduce the video teaching.

WATCH. This page provides space to take notes on the video teaching.

DISCUSS. This page includes questions and statements that guide the group to respond to the Kendricks' video teaching and to explore relevant Bible passages.

Personal Study

Each week provides five days of Bible study and learning activities for individual engagement between group sessions. The personal study revisits stories, Scriptures, and themes introduced in the video teaching so that participants can understand and apply them on a personal level. The days are numbered 1–5 to provide personal reading and activities for each day of the week, leaving two days off to worship with your church family and to meet as a small group. If your group meets on the same day as your worship gathering, use the extra day to reflect on what God is teaching you and to practice putting the biblical principles into action.

Day 5 of each week's personal study includes an exercise asking you to summarize the five key points you've learned over the past week.

Begin by listing five benefits you hope to gain from this Bible study.

1.

2.

3.

4.

5.

ABOUT THE MOVIE
OVERCOMER

MEET JOHN.

When circumstances beyond his control unravel the name he has built for himself, John Harrison "becomes the least likely coach helping the least likely runner attempt the impossible in the biggest race of the year."[1]

AFFIRM Films A Sony Company © 2019 CTMG.

MEET HANNAH.

She's on a journey of discovery. Like most adolescents, she wants to know where she came from, what she's good at, what it means to be part of a family, and where real value is found in life. Those are questions about identity.

AFFIRM Films A Sony Company © 2019 CTMG.

Life changes overnight for coach John Harrison when his high-school basketball team's state-championship dreams are crushed under the weight of unexpected news. When the largest manufacturing plant in town suddenly shuts down and hundreds of families begin moving away, John must come to grips with the challenges facing his family and his team. Urged by the school's principal to fill in and coach a sport he doesn't know or like, John is frustrated and questions his worth until he crosses paths with a student struggling with her own journey.

Filled with a powerful mix of faith, a twist of humor, and a ton of heart, the Kendrick brothers return to theaters with *OVERCOMER,* their newest feature following *FACING THE GIANTS, FIREPROOF, COURAGEOUS,* and the number one box-office hit *WAR ROOM.* The inspiring family film stars Alex Kendrick, Priscilla Shirer, Shari Rigby, Cameron Arnett, and introduces Aryn Wright-Thompson. *OVERCOMER* dares to leave you filled with hope, inspired to dream, and asks the question, What do you allow to define you?

FOR MORE ABOUT THE MOVIE, PLEASE VISIT
OVERCOMERMOVIE.COM

1. Jeannie Law, "New Kendrick Bros. Movie 'OVERCOMER' Based on Finding One's Identity in God, Stars Priscilla Shirer," *The Christian Post,* August 3, 2018, https://www.christianpost.com/news/kendrick-brothers-movie-overcomer-based-on-finding-identity-in-god-stars-priscilla-shirer-226556/.

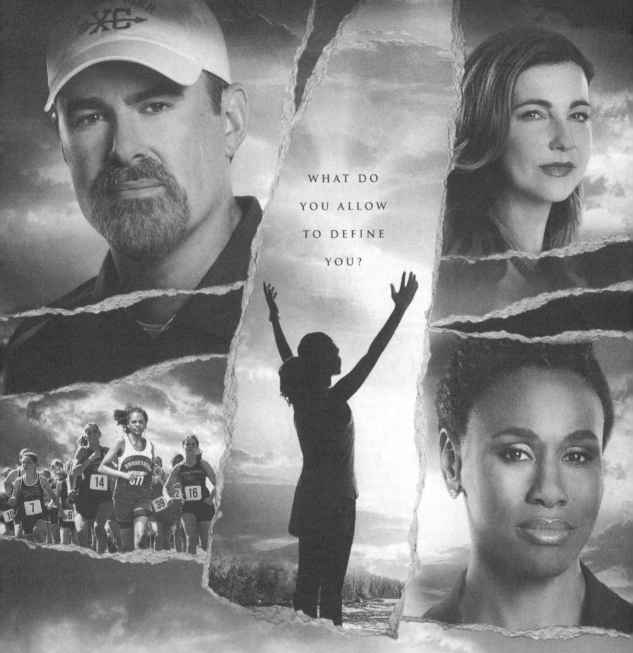

Week 1

CREATED
BY GOD

Start

Welcome to week 1 of *Defined*. We hope this Bible study changes your life in many ways, most specifically in the way you see your identity. We can't wait to hear how God works in and through you.

Let's take a moment to get to know one another before we watch this week's video.

Tell us your name and something about yourself.

Why did you choose to share that information about yourself? (Was it unique? Something you shared in common with others in the group? Just based on other people's answers?)

What are some common ways to define identity?

What do you hope to gain from this study of identity?

Through this study you'll learn what God's Word says about who you are and how to live out your true identity.

Take a moment to pray with your group. Pray that God will teach you through the group sessions and the personal studies. Pray that everyone in your group will have open hearts and minds. Pray that God will unify you as a group and will help you be vulnerable in sharing with one another for the next eight weeks. Thank Him for the opportunity to study His Word together.

After praying, watch the video teaching.

Watch

Use this section to take notes as you watch video session 1.

We don't want to let changing things determine our identity.

We have to be really careful that we don't let feelings determine what we believe about ourselves.

Four Rights God Has to Declare Who You Are

1. He created you.

2. God owns us.

3. God has authority.

4. God knows us better than anyone.

The Creator gets to define His creation.

God lovingly, intentionally, and wisely designed and made each one of us in His image on purpose for His glory.

Everybody is God-planned.

Discuss

After viewing the video, discuss the following questions with your group.

What points in the video were most significant for you?

What are some influences other than God's Word that try to define us? How does each of those false definitions result in bondage?

Read Genesis 1:26-28; Psalm 24:1; 139:1-4,16; Isaiah 64:8; 1 Corinthians 6:19-20. What do these verses reveal about God's right to define your life? What do they reveal about your identity?

What does it mean for people to be created in the image of God *(imago Dei)?* What do we share in common? How are we unique?

What freedoms and benefits come from embracing God's design for life? What are some consequences of rejecting God's design?

On a scale of 1 to 10 (1 being trash and 10 being treasure), how valuable do you secretly believe you are? With what value do you treat other people around you?

What part of your life or family is the hardest detail to thank God for? How could God use even your broken and painful experiences for good? Even if you don't currently see how something could be used for good, what has today's teaching emphasized about your life?

In what ways has this session been encouraging, convicting, or well timed?

After discussion, close the session with prayer.

Day 1
WHO IS GOD?

The opening chapters of the Bible present the beginning of life from two per-spectives. In fact, the title of the first book of the Bible, Genesis, is taken from the very first word in the original Hebrew language, meaning "beginning" or "origin." Chapter 1 of Genesis is a grand, sweeping overview, as though a camera were zoomed out as far as we could imagine, drawing closer and closer as creation grows increasingly complex. In chapter 2 we jump to a close-up scene within the story that we'll examine in more depth tomorrow. For now don't rush past the opening chapter. Don't even rush past the opening words. This isn't an introduction you can omit to get to the real story. This is the opening scene of the same story you're living in today. This is where it all begins—literally.

Record Genesis 1:1 either from memory or after looking it up.

What's significant about this first sentence in the Bible? Record all this sentence teaches us about God, ourselves, and life in general.

God:

Ourselves:

Life:

Use the chart to record what God created on each day in Genesis 1.

Day 1 (vv. 3-5)	Day 2 (vv. 6-8)	Day 3 (vv. 9-13)
Day 4 (vv. 14-19)	Day 5 (vv. 20-23)	Day 6 (vv. 24-31)

Has it ever occurred to you just how unthinkable it is that light was created on the first day, but the sun, moon, and stars weren't created until the fourth day? Light existed before what we consider the sources of light. But in God's infinite wisdom even His creation revealed information about Himself to us (see Rom. 1:20). The first three days established natural domains, and then God gave living creatures dominion to "be fruitful, multiply" (Gen. 1:22), filling each of those environments.

What does the repeated pattern of "Then God said. … And it was so" teach you about God, ourselves, and life in general?

God:
Ourselves:
Life:

What does the repeated declaration of "It was good" teach you about God, ourselves, and life in general?

God:
Ourselves:
Life:

What does the repeated blessing of "Be fruitful, multiply" teach you about God, ourselves, and life in general?

God:
Ourselves:
Life:

You can't know who you are without first knowing who God is. The Bible starts with the account of creation, not merely for the order of events but also for the foundation of truth. He isn't just the Creator. He's your Creator, and you're His good creation.

Conclude today's personal study by reflecting on the following prayer from God's Word. Take a moment to praise your Creator for who He is and for how much He loves you.

> *Grace to you and peace from God our Father and the Lord Jesus Christ …,*
> *who has blessed us with every spiritual blessing in the heavens in Christ.*
> EPHESIANS 1:2-3

Day 2
WHO AM I?

How would you describe yourself? What defines your identity?

Following the epic account of the first six days of creation, Genesis 2 zooms in for a close-up of the first man and woman as they opened their eyes to behold the miracle of life. The Lord God, who had just spoken light, planets, and every living and nonliving thing into existence, now changed the rhythm. It was no longer "God said, 'Let there be …'"

The LORD God formed the man out of the dust from the ground and breathed the breath of life into his nostrils, and the man became a living being.
GENESIS 2:7

The LORD God made the rib he had taken from the man into a woman and brought her to the man.
GENESIS 2:22

In the intimate account of their creation, God breathed life into man's nostrils and personally shaped the man and woman from earth and bone. The personal relationship between God and humanity became unmistakably clear. You aren't just one more part of the natural order:

God created man in his own image;
he created him in the image of God;
he created them male and female.
GENESIS 1:27

Why is it important to know that men and women are created in the image of God? What dignity and worth come from our relationship to God?

The image of God doesn't designate just a physical resemblance. The word *image* literally means "icon." Men and women represent God and relate to Him in a way that's different from all other created beings. All human beings from Adam and Eve onward are created to know and relate to God. Each person is a unique and beloved creation of God. Look at what Ephesians says later in the Bible:

> *We are his workmanship, created in Christ Jesus for good works.*
> EPHESIANS 2:10

If God specifically created you for His good purpose, what can't be true about your life? What has to be true about your life?

You possess a soul that enables you to know God in a way that's different from animals, plants, mountains, and all other created things. Your soul gives you a capacity to enter a personal relationship with your Father. Wrapped up in your identity is your responsibility to represent God and demonstrate His rule and reign over all creation (see Gen. 1:28). You've been created for a purpose. You can trust that whatever God's plan is for your life, you're perfectly suited for the work.

Now you probably want to know what you're supposed to *do*. What's God's plan for your life? The truth is that God first wants you to know who He created you to *be*. When you know who you are, you'll know how to act. Without understanding your identity, you aimlessly fumble around no matter what you do.

Identity is everything. Who you are matters. In fact, it matters every day. And who God is defines your identity. *Who* you are is determined by *whose* you are:

> *I have called you by your name; you are mine.*
> ISAIAH 43:1

How does believing you were created by God and belong to Him affect the way you see yourself? How does it affect the way you see your life?

Before your mind starts racing toward all the things you need to do, pause and thank God for everything He has already done. Conclude your time of personal study by declaring that you're His and that therefore you trust in His plan for your life.

Day 3
WHEN DID GOD BECOME INVOLVED IN OUR LIVES?

We are his workmanship, created in Christ Jesus for good
works, which God prepared ahead of time for us to do.
EPHESIANS 2:10

There's a reason we started this week's study with the first sentence in the Bible. It not only shows us that God is absolutely supreme—that He existed before all things and all things exist by the power of His will—but also points to the reality that we aren't accidents, afterthoughts, or abandoned ideas. God has been involved in our lives since the beginning of time. That doesn't mean He cared only about Adam and Eve, whom He fashioned by hand. He also knit each of us together, every intricate detail, in our mothers' wombs.

God has an intimate relationship with all people even before they're born. Psalm 139 beautifully addresses this reality, but there's a distinction between agreeing with this truth and embracing it as something that's true about you.

Read Psalm 139:1-6. Respond to the questions with details from your life.

What time did you wake up today?

Where will/did you go today?

Whom did/will you talk to today?

Read Psalm 139:7-12. Respond to the questions with details from your life.

Where do you live?

What are your favorite places to go?

When do you feel anxious or insignificant?

When do you feel most confident and alive?

Read Psalm 139:13-18. Respond to the questions with details from your life.

    Describe your physical appearance.

    Describe any physical limitations.

    When and where were you born?

    Describe your home life growing up.

    Describe your life now.

Read Psalm 139:19-22. Respond to the questions with details from your life.

    What hypocrisy do you hate in yourself or in others?

    What tragedies have you endured?

    What injustices have you witnessed?

Read Psalm 139:23-24. Respond to the questions with details from your life.

    What sin or hypocrisy needs to be confessed and removed from your life?

    Describe your current relationship with God.

    Describe your desired relationship with God.

The most important fact about you is that God created you. The second most important fact about you is that God created you wonderfully:

> *I will give thanks to You, for I am fearfully and wonderfully made;*
> *Wonderful are Your works,*
> *And my soul knows it very well.*
> PSALM 139:14, NASB

To conclude your time of study, review Psalm 139 verse by verse as a personal prayer, using the details you recorded during today's reflection.

Day 4
HOW IS GOD INVOLVED IN OUR LIVES?

God created us, has a plan for our lives, and has never abandoned His personal involvement in our lives. He always has been, always is, and always will be accomplishing His great purpose. In day 2 we saw that God's first desire is for us to know who we are. When we look at Scripture, we see that God gave Adam not only an identity but also a place, a partner, provision, a purpose, and parameters. When we recognize God's careful intention, we start to realize how important our God-given identity really is.

> **Read Genesis 2:4-9. What do we learn about the place God prepared for Adam? What does this place teach us about God? What does it teach us about Adam?**

> **Read Genesis 2:15-25. What purpose did God give Adam? What does this purpose teach us about the relationship between God and Adam?**

Our identity is formed by the place God puts us in and the purpose He gives to us. God placed people in a position of dominion so that we can join Him in His work of bringing life and order in the world. The garden and the call to do meaningful work came before the fall. God created us to thrive and flourish as He intended, to know Him personally, and to trust Him fully. The place and purpose God has given to all of us reveal His desire to be intimately involved in our lives.

> **What does the fact that God gave Adam work, a partner, and instructions in a perfect garden teach you about your identity and purpose?**

Like our place and purpose, God's design for our partner came before the fall. Adam didn't request a wife; rather, God gave Adam a partner out of His own goodness. God deeply cares about our relationships with other people. He defines who we are and gives us all we need to live out our identity. His purposeful intention is evident in the parameters God sets for our lives.

> **Read the apostle Paul's words to the people of Athens in Acts 17:22-34. How would you describe God's involvement in human lives since the beginning with Adam and Eve? How and why has He been working?**

> **How does Paul's teaching on false beliefs about God address your own tendencies in today's culture, even without physical shrines and idols?**

God doesn't need us to serve Him; He isn't helpless without us or dependent on us (see v. 25). We aren't expected to work *for* God. We're invited to work *with* God within the parameters He has set. He's continually involved in our lives and invites us to follow Him into fullness of life. The LORD God is at work *in* us and all *around* us, and He desires to work *through* us as well. Primarily, we join God in His work when we seek to know Him and point others toward Him.

> **How could God be working around and through you, providing ways to join Him in bringing abundant life, order, and flourishing to your area of influence?**

Conclude your time of personal study by considering the ways God is at work in your life, whatever your work and routine may be. Ask Him for courage to trust and obey Him completely. Pray for opportunities to share the truth about your Creator and LORD God with others so that they can know Him too.

Day 5
TAKE FIVE: LIFE

Record the five main takeaways God taught you through the group session and personal studies this week. You may want to choose one truth from each day, or certain days may have been especially meaningful to you.

1.

2.

3.

4.

5.

Just as each person's hand is created in the same way but has unique fingerprints, God's Word remains the same, but each person hears and applies it in specific ways at different seasons in his or her life. Your DNA, the shape of your ear, the pattern in the iris of your eye, the combination of your physical features, the stride of your walk are all unique to you as an individual. You're skillfully and wonderfully made— one of a kind. But the common bond we all share as human beings is that we're created in the image of God.

In the movie business the phrase "Take five" means to take a short break of approximately five minutes. As you complete this study, it's important that you take a break, not just to relax from studying but to reflect on what you've been studying. Don't rush through the content each week. Pause to consider some key takeaways. What are the main truths you need to retain in order to have a good grasp of each week's topic? What was most significant? What challenged, convicted, or encouraged you?

This time can be as brief or as long as you need it to be. The aim is to identify truths you don't want to forget—truths you want to take with you when you move on to the next part of this study and, most important, to the next phase of your life.

Look at the natural world around you. God's fingerprints are all over it:

The heavens declare the glory of God,
and the expanse proclaims the work of his hands.
Day after day they pour out speech;
night after night they communicate knowledge.
There is no speech; there are no words;
their voice is not heard.
Their message has gone out to the whole earth,
and their words to the ends of the world.
In the heavens he has pitched a tent for the sun.
It is like a bridegroom coming from his home;
it rejoices like an athlete running a course.
PSALM 19:1-5

Read Psalm 19 in your Bible. Let it guide a time of prayerful reflection.

Week 2

BROKEN
BY SIN

Start

In each group session we'll start by reviewing what we learned in the previous week's personal studies. Refer to your notes in week 1, especially day 5, when answering these questions with the group.

What new truth did you learn, or what stood out to you over the past week?

What did you learn about God from the story of creation (day 1)?

What did you learn about your identity and the image of God (day 2)?

Did you end the week feeling more, less, or equally confident about who you are as fearfully and wonderfully made for God's purpose?

So far God's Word has established the foundational truth that we're all created in God's image. Now we need to admit that we're broken as individuals and as the entire human race. Although God created us, a dramatic turn took place, and we're now separated from Him.

Today is going to be like a descent on a roller coaster; we're going to dive into a dark hole and then come back up again later. For the good news of the gospel to truly thrill our hearts, we first have to feel the gravity of our sin.

Pray for God to work in everyone's heart as you prepare to hear from His Word.

After praying, watch the video teaching.

Watch

Use this section to take notes as you watch video session 2.

Rejecting God's ways, His Word, and His design brings sin, and sin ultimately leads to death.

Our hearts are fickle, and they might be leading us in the wrong direction.

Our hearts, at the core, are still wicked and broken before God.

God has not abandoned us in our brokenness and sin.

Anyone who is willing to repent and call upon Jesus and believe in Him can be saved and forgiven. They can experience a new identity, and their lives can be transformed.

God took the initiative to send Jesus to save us, and He's inviting us to call upon Him wherever we are.

You, in God's eyes, are a brand-new creation.

Discuss

After viewing the video, discuss the following questions with your group.

List some examples of brokenness you see in the world. What examples of brokenness have you experienced in your life?

Ask people if they can collectively name the Ten Commandments. Read Exodus 20:1-17 to identify this basic list. Read Matthew 5:21-22 to add Jesus' interpretation of the law.

Using only the Ten Commandments and Jesus' rule for interpretation, how many of you are guilty of breaking any commandments today? How many times do you think you've broken them this week? In your life?

At what point in your life did you become aware of your inability to change your own sinful heart? What happened to make you aware of this reality?

If you're comfortable sharing, what sin most clearly revealed your brokenness, and how did it contribute to a misunderstanding of your identity? How does Christ fulfill the desire that you were seeking to satisfy with a pattern of sin?

How would you describe the nature of sin, based on the Scriptures presented in the video?

What steps were provided in the video for dealing with sin in our lives?

In what ways has this session been encouraging, convicting, or well timed?

After discussion, close the session with prayer.

Day 1
THE PROBLEM IN OUR NATURE

Last week you studied the creation of the world and of men and women in particular. After speaking the universe into existence, as well as everything in heaven and on earth, God personally created the first man and woman, breathing His own breath of life into their nostrils. Adam and Eve woke up in paradise with all they needed to enjoy life together. They were blessed and told to be fruitful and multiply, filling the earth with the image of God and reflecting His good dominion throughout His creation. Think about it:

- Their relationships with God—perfect.
- Their relationships with each other—perfect.
- Their relationship with the natural world—perfect.

What could be better? What could go wrong? Obviously, something went terribly wrong.

Read Genesis 3:1. What can you learn from this verse about the nature of temptation and sin?

Read Genesis 3:2-5. What can you learn about the nature of temptation and sin from the serpent's response to God's command?

Read Genesis 2:9; 3:6-7. What did every tree share in common? What does that commonality reveal about the nature of God's provision and your obedience?

What was the only unique trait of the forbidden fruit and its result? What does that trait reveal about the nature of temptation and sin?

Finish the story by reading Genesis 3:8-24. Record the characteristics that stand out most to you about the altered nature of human life.

Although Adam and Eve's disobedience brought brokenness into every aspect of human life, the LORD God came to them, called them, and clothed them. Did you notice that sending them out of the garden was an act of grace? God protected them from the tree of life, whose fruit would have resulted in an eternity of brokenness. In their shame He had a plan for salvation.

After sin entered the world through human disobedience, work became difficult, and life became painful. Relationships were characterized by brokenness and blame. Individuals felt shame and fear. These conditions became the new normal. However, the following realities didn't change: God's love for us, His desire for a relationship with us, and our identities as bearers of His image.

Would you describe yourself as currently hiding from God or seeking Him? Why should you seek God and never hide, no matter what you've done?

God's commands reveal God's character. Doubting His commands is the equivalent of doubting His character. When He prohibits something, it's because He has provided better things. The serpent's question "Did God really say …?" (v. 1) was a temptation to doubt God's goodness and to break the relationship with Him. God's question "Where are you?" (v. 9) was an invitation to trust His goodness and to restore the relationship with Him. Do you hear Him? No matter how far you've run from Him or how long you've walked with Him, He's calling you closer. Trust Him. He's good. Always.

Conclude your study today by seeking God in prayer—confessing sin, surrendering shame, and trusting the goodness of God's character as you listen for His voice in His commands.

Day 2
THE PROBLEM
IN OUR HEARTS

"Follow your heart." You've surely heard this advice before. Maybe you've even said it. When you realize that something is wrong with you and that life is utterly broken, the mantra of our culture is to let your heart be your guide. This conventional wisdom permeates nearly every TV show, movie, and song.

It sounds great. It almost sounds spiritual. Well-meaning Christians occasionally offer this advice. We all tend to believe it. But there's a problem.

Your heart.

Record Jeremiah 17:9, personalizing the verse by replacing the first word, *The*, with *My*.

The problem with following your heart is that your heart is the problem. In the garden of Eden, Adam and Eve knew the truth. They knew the fruit of every other tree was beautiful, delicious, and free to enjoy. The problem wasn't ignorance. It was selfishness. They had no reason to doubt God's command, yet they were tempted to doubt His character. They wondered whether God was keeping something desirable from them. They wanted what would literally kill them. When the serpent's lie twisted the desires of the first man and woman and they took bites of the God-forbidden fruit, nightmarish shame rushed through their veins and washed over their naked bodies.

Sin has infected the heart of every child born of a man and a woman since that day. Every person is now born with a sinful nature. The entire human race—every tribe, tongue, and nation—has inherited this shared family trait. But before you play the victim card, claiming it's not your fault that you were born with a broken heart bent dangerously inward with pride, look at what God's Word has to say about everyone's nature and everyone's choices.

Record Proverbs 14:12.

Read James 1:13-17. Adam blamed Eve or God for his sin. Eve blamed the serpent. What did James say about God's relation to sin (see v. 13)? What did he say about God's character and interaction with us (see v. 17)?

Record James 1:14, personalizing the verse by replacing generic phrases like "each person is," "he is," and "his" with "I am" and "my."

Read James 1:15. In the beginning God blessed Adam and Eve to be fruitful and multiply. How did James describe the reproductive process of evil?

Following your heart leads away from God because the problem begins in your heart. You want what will kill you. You don't trust that God—your Creator—wants what's best for you. Your own desire overwhelms your knowledge of Him, and you choose to sin, believing the lie that it will be worth it. But it never is. Desire becomes sin, and sin becomes death, just as God warned in the garden. The pattern continues without exception.

Everybody has the same problem. Everybody has the same choice. It's your turn right now. Will you make excuses and pass the blame? Will you continue to let your heart be tempted by things you know aren't good for you?

The fact is that you're sinful by nature and by choice. But it's also a fact that God is gracious and good. Unlike the fickle desires of your heart, He never changes. Your best efforts to fix your own problems and the problems in the world by following your heart are as ineffective as Adam and Eve's attempt to hide from the Creator behind trees and fig leaves that He created. He spoke the universe into existence. Did they really think He didn't know where they were or what they had done? Do you really believe following the desires of your own heart will turn out any better than it did for Adam and Eve?

Conclude your study with honesty before God. Silence may be appropriate for a while as the Father of lights begins to reveal dark spots in your heart. Allow yourself to feel the foolishness of trusting your own desires rather than the wisdom of your Creator, the giver of "every good and perfect gift" (Jas. 1:17).

Day 3
THE PROBLEM IN OUR SIN

This is a heavy week, but don't give up. There's a light at the end of the tunnel, but you have to move through the darkness to experience the joy of freedom on the other side.

As we saw yesterday, the same root of sin has corrupted every human heart. The diagnosis is terminal. There's no cure. Even Jesus' half brother James affirmed that the problem of sin is fatal. After generations of so-called human progress, people still can't fill the gaping holes in their hearts. The problem of sin remains. Broken people can't fix themselves:

> *"Absolute futility," says the Teacher.*
> *"Absolute futility. Everything is futile."*
> **ECCLESIASTES 1:2**

That conclusion is repeated throughout the Book of Ecclesiastes. Most of the things the Teacher experimented with in his pursuit of wisdom, the various desires of his heart, weren't bad things. Nevertheless, all the wealth, pleasure, discipline, education, work, relationships, and experiences in the world can't provide meaning, purpose, or identity.

List several pursuits in which you've tried to find satisfaction and identity. Consider various stages of your life—different ages, interests, and priorities.

Draw a star beside anything on your list that you use to define your identity.

Your heart can be enticed by the pursuits you listed—even inherently good pursuits like work, family, or church—to define your identity and purpose in life. When you desire something to do for you what only God can do, it becomes a potential idol, false god, and futile pursuit. Not everything you enjoy, desire, or feel is sinful or deceptive. God gave you a heart, not just a mind. He created beauty and pleasure for your enjoyment. He's the giver of "every good and perfect gift" (Jas. 1:17). Every tree in the garden of Eden was a delight to the eye and good for food. The problem is when your desires tempt you to put those things in God's place or to put yourself in God's place as the judge of what's best for yourself. That's the heart of sin.

Read Romans 1:18-25 and summarize the human problem in personal terms. What happened to humanity's relationship with the Creator?

Though the problem is universal, it manifests itself in many different ways. Your temptation and sin may not be the same as your neighbor's or a family member's. The following list of sins is so bracing and varied that anyone who's honest can't keep from finding himself or herself in it. We're all broken. That's not an excuse. It's a wake-up call.

Highlight all of the sins in the following verses that you've been guilty of at any time in your life.

Because they did not think it worthwhile to acknowledge God, God delivered them over to a corrupt mind so that they do what is not right. They are filled with all unrighteousness, evil, greed, and wickedness. They are full of envy, murder, quarrels, deceit, and malice. They are gossips, slanderers, God-haters, arrogant, proud, boastful, inventors of evil, disobedient to parents, senseless, untrustworthy, unloving, and unmerciful. Although they know God's just sentence—that those who practice such things deserve to die—they not only do them, but even applaud others who practice them.
ROMANS 1:28-32

The person who keeps all of the laws except one is as guilty as a person who has broken all of God's laws.
JAMES 2:10, NLT

Conclude your time of personal study with prayerful reflection and confession. Admit specific sin by name, recognizing that any and every sin is a serious problem. Before you can live in the good news of the gospel, you have to identify with the bad news of sin—not just generally but specifically. Even if you're already a Christian, being reminded of the deceptive nature of your own desires and the unique ways they creep into your life is vital to your spiritual health and growth. Pray now, confessing your sins.

Day 4
THE LEVEL
PLAYING FIELD

Any choice you make reveals what you truly believe to be right, at least what's right for you, as some people would say. The option you decided to act on is the one you determined to be best, whether it's a multiple-choice question, a new purchase, a change in jobs, lying, cheating, or stealing. This is the way everybody acts. Even if you know it's a bad idea, some nagging desire convinces you that it could work out this time. The risk feels worth it.

> *All a person's ways seem right to him,*
> *but the LORD weighs hearts.*
> **PROVERBS 21:2**

Your various sins are symptoms of a deadly heart problem. Each day this week has probed a bit deeper into your own issues, moving from the general sin nature common among all people to unique manifestations of sin specific to your life. The diagnosis is fatal. Treating the symptoms by trying harder to do good works can't fix the problem of sin in your heart. You have to be exposed in your shame and allow your Creator to restore you. Until you realize you have a problem, you'll never stop hiding and following your heart:

> *You were dead in your trespasses and sins in which you previously lived*
> *according to the ways of this world, according to the ruler of the power of the*
> *air, the spirit now working in the disobedient. We too all previously lived*
> *among them in our fleshly desires, carrying out the inclinations of our flesh and*
> *thoughts, and we were by nature children under wrath as the others were also.*
> **EPHESIANS 2:1-3**

The sickness of sinful hearts doesn't lead only to eventual physical death. How would you summarize the diagnosis of the problem in the previous Scriptures?

Paul diagnosed the problem this way:

> *All have sinned and fall short of the glory of God.*
> ROMANS 3:23

Rewrite this verse as a personal confession, using *I* instead of *All*.

A popular expression says the ground is level at the foot of the cross. In sports the expression is "to level the playing field." Those sayings mean no person or player has an advantage over anyone else. By now you've seen that we all have the same need—salvation. We need saving from ourselves. We need a miraculous change of heart.

Read Romans 3:9-30. How are all people described in these verses? How does that description make you feel?

Rewrite verse 24 as a personal confession, using "I am" instead of "They are."

Fortunately, God did not leave you in Romans 3:23 to your own failed rebellion. The good news of the gospel is truly wonderful once you recognize the desperately bad news of sin. Conclude your study by using the following psalm as your prayer. Thank God that He hasn't left you helpless in your sin with a dead heart. He has come to you in Christ, the Great Physician. Listen for His voice. Follow Him.

> *Search me, God, and know my heart;*
> *test me and know my concerns.*
> *See if there is any offensive way in me;*
> *lead me in the everlasting way.*
> PSALM 139:23-24

Day 5
TAKE FIVE: SIN

Record the five main takeaways God taught you through the group session and personal studies this week. You may want to choose one truth from each day, or certain days may have been especially meaningful to you.

1.

2.

3.

4.

5.

A psalm is provided on day 5 each week to help you prayerfully reflect on the biblical truth related to each week's topic. Psalms has been called the prayer book of the Bible. As you read these prayers, you can relate to the full range of human emotions that are expressed with amazing honesty. In various psalms the writer's hands are reverently folded, clapping in praise, reaching in desperation, waving in surrender, open in petition, or clenched in angry fists.

Assume a posture that allows you to physically express your heart to the Lord now. A good exercise for today may be to squeeze your hands tightly, symbolic of a sinful heart clinging to its own desires. As you confess your sins in prayer, open your hands toward the floor, symbolic of placing your sin and your entire life before God. Next turn your palms upward, symbolic of your humble willingness to receive His grace and His will for your life in Christ. Finally, lift your hands in surrender and praise, proclaiming that you'll fully trust in His goodness and follow Him wherever He leads.

Read the following passage as you consider the weight of your sin.

Be gracious to me, God,
according to your faithful love;
according to your abundant compassion,
blot out my rebellion.
Completely wash away my guilt
and cleanse me from my sin.
For I am conscious of my rebellion,
and my sin is always before me.
Against you—you alone—I have sinned
and done this evil in your sight.
So you are right when you pass sentence;
you are blameless when you judge.
Indeed, I was guilty when I was born;
I was sinful when my mother conceived me.
PSALM 51:1-5

Read Psalm 51 in your Bible. Let it guide a time of prayerful reflection.

Week 3

TRANSFORMED BY THE GOSPEL

START

We'll start by reviewing what we learned in the previous week's personal studies. Refer to your notes in week 2, especially day 5, when answering these questions with the group.

What new truth did you learn, or what stood out to you this week?

In what ways did you see sin differently this week (day 1)?

What was your response to the idea of following your heart (day 2)?

What were your thoughts about the hand exercise during prayer (day 5)?

Did you end the week more, less, or equally aware of the presence of sin?

Week 1 slowly developed our understanding of our identity as people created in the image of God, while week 2 described humanity's sudden fall from God in sin. This week will present the equally dramatic upturn of the gospel. We promised light at the end of the tunnel, and this week we'll experience the liberating thrill of salvation.

Pray that God will guide the group through His Word as you trace the change that happens when God moves in human hearts and people receive the gospel.

After praying, watch the video teaching.

Watch

_____

Use this section to take notes as you watch video session 3.

God doesn't just forgive us. He completely transforms us.

Our identity shifts when we give our lives to Christ.

Because of our sinfulness, we deserve God's judgment, and we are under God's wrath.

Before Christ

1. Dead in sin
2. Enslaved to lust
3. Children of God's wrath
4. Separate from Christ
5. No hope without God
6. Strangers and aliens

Grace is a free gift, given to the undeserved, of exactly what they need.

Wherever we go, the Holy Spirit is inside us. We get to be a holy of holies of God.

Before Christ	In Christ
Dead in sin	Alive in Christ
Enslaved to lust	Free (John 8:36)
Children of wrath	Justified (Rom. 8:1)
Separated from God (Matt. 27:46)	A dwelling place of God
A hopeless future	A hope of heaven (Phil. 3:20)
Without God	Brought near
Stranger	Part of God's family (Eph. 2:19)

Discuss

After viewing the video, discuss the following questions with your group.

On the video several Scriptures were read and statements were made about the transformation that occurs in our lives through the gospel. What was the nature of our lives before Christ saved us? What's our transformed nature in Christ?

Read Ephesians 2:1-5,8-10. Identify one essential part of the gospel message included in each verse.

Using your summary of the teaching in Ephesians 2, can someone put those points together to share a simple gospel message?

How would you explain the difference between the root of salvation and the fruit of salvation?

Review the seven evidences of salvation. Why is each one important?
1. Obedience
2. The Son
3. Repentance
4. Discipline
5. Love
6. Spirit
7. Jesus

If time allows, encourage people to share when and how Christ transformed their lives through saving faith in the gospel.

After discussion, close the session with prayer.

Day 1
RECLAIMED

The Book of Ephesians is a powerful little book. Only six chapters long, it's divided in half, with the first three chapters focusing on our identity in Christ and the last three chapters turning the focus to how we live out this new identity. Character and commands. Our position in Christ determines our practice of Christian living. Indicatives (statements about who you are) are foundational for the imperatives (statements about what you should do).

This week you'll turn your attention from your old identity to your new identity in Christ.

Read Ephesians 2:1-5 and use verses 4-5 to fill in the blanks below.

But _____, who is _____ in _____,

because of his great _____ that he had for us,

made us _____ with _____

Even though we were _____ in _____.

You are _____ by _____!

Rewrite Ephesians 2:1-3, personalizing it by using "I was" and "my" instead of "you were" and "your." These exercises make the truth of Scripture seem real, as if God's Word is alive in your life instead of remaining an idea in a book about people in general.

Rewrite Ephesians 2:4, personalizing it by using *me* instead of *us*.

Rewrite Ephesians 2:5, personalizing it by using "I am" instead of "You are."

When you were dead in trespasses and in the uncircumcision of your
flesh, he made you alive with him and forgave us all our trespasses. He
erased the certificate of debt, with its obligations, that was against us
and opposed to us, and has taken it away by nailing it to the cross.
COLOSSIANS 2:13-14

The wages of sin is death, but the gift of God
is eternal life in Christ Jesus our Lord.
ROMANS 6:23

What did God do to transform your identity by His grace? How did He bring you to life when you were spiritually dead? What happened to the curse of sin?

God warned Adam in the garden that sin would result in death. You've seen that both spiritual death and physical death were consequences of his sin. When you read the words *trespasses* or *debt*, imagine that you've entered a garden despite warning signs and have eaten fruit that wasn't yours. You've trespassed and incurred a debt. The bigger problem is that once it's happened, it can't be undone. You can't put the fruit back or promise never to do it again. A price has to be paid.

When you chose to make your own decisions regardless of what God said, you earned the same penalty as Adam, Eve, and every person since their initial rebellion. You desired to be your own boss and incurred a debt you could never repay. The wages earned for all the hard work you've done to satisfy your desires was death. Sin is a cruel, unforgiving master. But the wage is fair. It was earned. People are owed what they've worked for.

Jesus paid the debt you owed. He bought you back out of slavery from your own desires. He died on the cross so that you could receive eternal life instead. There's no removing the nail to take back your debt. It's finished. Settled. Paid in full. Conclude your study today by praising God for erasing your debt and giving you freedom and new life in Christ.

Day 2
RENEWED

*If anyone is in Christ, he is a new creation; the old
has passed away, and see, the new has come!*
2 CORINTHIANS 5:17

The apostle Paul loved to talk about being in Christ. He addressed this idea more than 160 times in his letters, which have been preserved as books in the New Testament. The theme of unity with Christ is so prevalent and the reality is so transformative that it would be reasonable to say it sums up the Christian life.

Nothing is more important than your relationship with God through faith in Christ. It changes everything. More precisely, *He* changes everything. In a vision of our future home given to John the disciple, Jesus announced from His eternal throne:

Look, I am making everything new.
REVELATION 21:5

This pronouncement shouldn't surprise us. John's Gospel tells us:

*In the beginning was the Word, and the Word was with God, and the Word
was God. He was with God in the beginning. All things were created through
him, and apart from him not one thing was created that has been created.*
JOHN 1:1-3

Notice that John didn't say Jesus will make all new things. He said Jesus will make all things new. Jesus is renewing His creation. Paul described the renewal of your identity as being conformed to the image of Christ (see Rom. 8:29). God created all things through Jesus in the beginning. Jesus will make all things new again in the end.

Read John 3:16-18. How do you become a new creation and receive eternal life in Christ?

Jesus provides renewal at the cross. The night before He was crucified, He gathered John and the other disciples to celebrate Passover. During the Passover meal Jews (the people of Israel) remembered God's act of salvation from their slavery in Egypt.

> *[Jesus] took the cup, after supper, and said, "This cup is the new covenant in my blood. Do this, as often as you drink it, in remembrance of me."*
> 1 CORINTHIANS 11:25

Telling His disciples to remember Him meant that He was God and was about to deliver His people from a greater slavery than Egypt, with more precious blood than a Passover lamb. When you're saved by believing in Jesus, you enter the new covenant.

Read Jeremiah 31:31-34. Describe five benefits of the new covenant in Christ.

1. It won't be _____ (v. 32).

2. The Lord will put _____
   and write it _____ (v. 33).

3. The Lord will be _____, and we will be
   _____ (v. 33).

4. We will _____ (v. 34).

5. He will _____
   and never _____ (v. 34).

Conclude today's study by remembering that *who* you are is defined by *whose* you are. When you're in Christ, you're part of the new covenant. You have a new spirit that replaces what was broken by sin and leads you to love and serve the Lord. Thank God now for your new heart, new spirit, and new identity in Christ. Use the following Scripture as a guide.

> *I will give you a new heart and put a new spirit within you;*
> *I will remove your heart of stone and give you a heart of flesh.*
> EZEKIEL 36:26

Day 3
REDIRECTED

A question you should ask yourself at this point is, *How can I tell whether I've truly believed in Jesus?* Believing in Jesus isn't the same as merely acknowledging that He existed. It's not even the same as admitting that He's the Son of God. Jesus transforms from the inside out. Believing in Jesus will always be evident in the way we live and the things we care about.

Since you've believed in Jesus, what has changed about your life?

John 3:16-18 explains that Christ came to save us, not to condemn us. Anyone who believes in Him is saved, and anyone who doesn't is already condemned. John went on to describe the difference between people who believe in Jesus and those who don't by using one of his favorite themes of light and darkness:

> *This is the judgment: The light has come into the world, and people loved darkness rather than the light because their deeds were evil. For everyone who does evil hates the light and avoids it, so that his deeds may not be exposed. But anyone who lives by the truth comes to the light, so that his works may be shown to be accomplished by God.*
> JOHN 3:19-21

What might it look like to love the light? What might it look like to hate the darkness?

If the goal of the Christian life is to be like Jesus, your desires will be redirected. What we want and desire should look like what Jesus wants and desires. Because Jesus is light, loving Jesus looks like loving the light, seeking to follow it, and leading other people to it. John continued the theme of light in His first letter to the church:

> *We are writing these things so that our joy may be complete. This is the message we have heard from him and declare to you: God is light, and there is absolutely no darkness in him. If we say, "We have fellowship with him," and yet we walk in darkness, we are lying and are not practicing the truth. If we walk in the light as he himself is in the light, we have fellowship with one another, and the blood of Jesus his Son cleanses us from all sin.*
>
> 1 JOHN 1:4-7

How does walking in the light strengthen our relationships with other people?

How could walking in the light motivate you to help other people find the light you've found?

Read 1 John 1:8–2:2. How would you use these verses to explain the gospel to someone?

How can you know the gospel is true and is working in your life? You have new desires. You love the light and hate the darkness. You follow God's commands to love Him and love others. Whoever belongs to God loves what God loves:

> *This is how we know that we know him: if we keep his commands. The one who says, "I have come to know him," and yet doesn't keep his commands, is a liar, and the truth is not in him. But whoever keeps his word, truly in him the love of God is made complete. This is how we know we are in him: The one who says he remains in him should walk just as he walked.*
>
> 1 JOHN 2:3-6

Conclude this lesson by reflecting on the gospel and the ways it has changed your heart. Your actions don't earn your salvation, but they reveal the desires of your heart. If people looked at your life, would they see Jesus? Are you following Him in a new direction?

Day 4
REPURPOSED

Today's study will build on the general idea of your new identity in Christ by identifying some practical characteristics of a new heart. What does it look like to turn away from the darkness, come out of hiding, and walk in the light with a heart like Jesus' heart?

> *I say then, walk by the Spirit and you will certainly not carry out the desire of the flesh. For the flesh desires what is against the Spirit, and the Spirit desires what is against the flesh; these are opposed to each other, so that you don't do what you want. But if you are led by the Spirit, you are not under the law.*
> GALATIANS 5:16-18

When you believe in Jesus, the Holy Spirit lives inside you. He's the One who enables you to want to follow light and shun darkness. He renews your heart. If you've ever felt the tension between your old self and your new self, don't mistake that struggle for the absence of a new heart. The fact that you feel opposition is a sign of good spiritual health; it means the Spirit is working inside you. When your sinful desires win out in the tug-of-war inside you, the key is to confess and repent. If you never feel resistance, you should question whether you're actually growing in Christ. Yet even growing Christians will occasionally feel a pull toward darkness.

Check any desires of the flesh that are still a struggle for you (see Gal. 5:19).

- ☐ **Sexual immorality**
- ☐ **Promiscuity**
- ☐ **Sorcery**
- ☐ **Strife**
- ☐ **Outbursts of anger**
- ☐ **Dissensions**
- ☐ **Envy**
- ☐ **Carousing**

- ☐ **Moral impurity**
- ☐ **Idolatry**
- ☐ **Hatreds**
- ☐ **Jealousy**
- ☐ **Selfish ambitions**
- ☐ **Factions**
- ☐ **Drunkenness**
- ☐ **Anything similar**

Read Galatians 5:22-23 and record the fruit of the Spirit on the following chart.

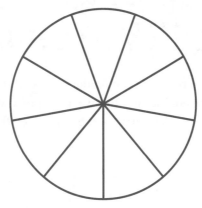

When we know the Spirit, He produces spiritual fruit in our lives. Notice that Galatians says "fruit" and not "fruits." This is an important distinction. The fruit of the Spirit is like the pieces of a single citrus fruit. A tree bears only one kind of fruit. There's no such thing as a generic citrus tree that produces oranges, lemons, and limes. But the inside of an orange, for example, reveals multiple pieces of the same fruit.

It would be tempting to say, "I'm not a lemon tree, so I need to produce only oranges." Spiritually, this argument would be like saying, "I'm not a kind person, so I need to have only self-control." The reality is that the nine distinct pieces make up a single fruit of the Holy Spirit in your life, so you don't get to pick and choose the fruit you exhibit. Of course, some traits will develop more easily for you. Other traits will develop more easily for others. But a healthy heart with the Spirit of Christ in it shouldn't have gaping holes. That would be rotten fruit.

Jesus said people can be recognized by their fruit (see Matt 7:16). The Holy Spirit at work in our lives gives us the freedom to deny sin and choose God. When this happens, we produce fruit. Freedom doesn't mean following your heart. True freedom is following the One who created and redeemed you—your Savior and Lord:

> *For freedom, Christ set us free. Stand firm then*
> *and don't submit again to a yoke of slavery.*
> **GALATIANS 5:1**

Pray that the Holy Spirit will help you weed out old desires of the flesh that still express themselves in your life and that He will help you grow into a well-rounded, Spirit-filled bearer of good fruit.

Day 5
TAKE FIVE: GOSPEL

Use the space below to record five main takeaways God taught you through the group session and personal studies this week. You may want to choose one truth from each day, or certain days may have been especially meaningful to you.

1.

2.

3.

4.

5.

A heart-wrenching story of grace is told in John 8:1-11. A woman had been caught in the act of adultery, dragged into public, and thrown into the dirt at Jesus' feet. She was every bit as naked as Adam and Eve had been but without even fig leaves to cover her guilty shame. The adulteress was exposed, and she had no way to hide from the eyes of her accusers and onlookers.

Instead of joining in their judgment, Jesus bent down and began writing in the dust with His finger. You can imagine that the stares were drawn away from the helpless woman and onto the merciful hands of Jesus. The Savior challenged the accusers, inviting anyone who wasn't guilty of their own sins to throw stones of judgment at her. They all walked away empty-handed before Jesus stood up again. Christ then told this woman that her sins were forgiven and to go live free from sin.

Consider the mercy Christ has shown you as you read the following passage.

*I waited patiently for the L*ORD*,*
and he turned to me and heard my cry for help.
He brought me up from a desolate pit,
out of the muddy clay,
and set my feet on a rock,
making my steps secure.
He put a new song in my mouth,
a hymn of praise to our God.
Many will see and fear,
*and they will trust in the L*ORD*.*
Let all who seek you rejoice and be glad in you;
let those who love your salvation continually say,
*"The L*ORD* is great!"*
I am oppressed and needy;
may the Lord think of me.
You are my helper and my deliverer;
my God, do not delay.
PSALM 40:1-3,16-17

Read Psalm 40 in your Bible. Let it guide a time of prayerful reflection.

WHO WE ARE IN CHRIST

Start

We'll start by reviewing what we learned in the previous week's personal studies. Refer to your notes in week 3, especially day 5, when answering these questions with the group.

What new truth did you learn, or what stood out to you this week?

What was the most sobering fact about life without Christ (day 1)?

How would you summarize the difference between knowing Jesus and knowing about Jesus (day 3)?

How have you experienced God working in you so far during this study?

This week we'll be immersed in the indicatives of our identity in Christ. We'll recognize the stark contrast in our lives before and after Christ and then examine Ephesians 1–2 to learn what God's Word declares about who we are. While week 1 taught us what the Bible says is true of all people, week 4 will focus on what's uniquely true of people who are in Christ.

After praying, watch the video teaching.

Watch

Use this section to take notes as you watch video session 4.

God, in His mercy and grace, has called us into life through Jesus Christ and has saved us, forgiven us, and made us His workmanship in Christ Jesus.

In Christ I am blessed with every spiritual blessing.

We're chosen, we're accepted, and we're beloved because we're in Christ.

Beloved means "one who is unconditionally loved with *agape* love by God."

God has adopted us.

We're redeemed, and we're forgiven.

I am sealed with the Holy Spirit.

The Holy Spirit's presence in our lives is the guarantee of our coming inheritance.

In Christ

1. I am blessed with every spiritual blessing.
2. I am chosen, accepted, and beloved.
3. I am a child of God.
4. I am redeemed and forgiven.
5. I am sealed with the Holy Spirit.

Instead of living in shame and guilt, you can know that God has changed your identity.

Discuss

After viewing the video, discuss the following questions with your group.

What points in the video were most significant for you?

What realities are true about all people? What realities are uniquely true about people who are in Christ?

Read Ephesians 1:1-14. Count the times phrases like "in Christ," "in him," or "in the Beloved One" are repeated. What was Paul emphasizing?

What's your general impression of this elaborate introduction to Paul's letter? How would you summarize the primary point Paul was making right away in his letter to the Ephesians? Why was he so intentional about this point to start his letter?

Review the passage and identify at least one truth about who we are in Christ that you find in each verse. Which truth stands out most to you? Why?

Read Ephesians 2:12-22. What dramatic transformations took place between who we once were and who we are now in Christ? Why is unity vital to who we are in Christ? In what way is the Christian identity both an individual and a collective identity?

How does your identity affect the way you—
• view God, yourself, your past, and your future?
• think, speak, act, treat others, and pray?
• handle success, failure, and loss?
• react to criticism and false accusations?
• respond to temptation and sin?

After discussion, close the session with prayer.

Day 1
I AM CHOSEN

Do you remember the days of games on the playground or in the neighborhood? Being a team captain came with a lot of power and responsibility. Whom did you choose? Did you choose the people you liked best? Did you choose the people who would play the game best? Did you get stuck with someone you didn't like or who was more of a liability than an asset to your team? The only thing better than choosing a fun or winning team was the feeling of being chosen as a member of that fun or winning team. You were valued before the game even started. You were chosen by the captain.

Read Ephesians 1:1. Whose choice defined Paul's identity?

Read Acts 9:1-22. How did this experience prove Paul's statement in Ephesians 1:1 about God's will for his life?

How can Paul's conversion story be a hopeful reminder when you doubt God's love for you because of something you've done?

Regardless of your performance—past, present, or future—you've been chosen by God, in Christ, for His purpose. Nothing could be more liberating and life-giving than that. Your failures and sins no longer define you. Who you are in Christ becomes the single most important distinguishing characteristic about you. Who you are is defined by who God's Word says you are.

Your Bible translation probably has multiple sentences for Ephesians 1:3-14, but when Paul originally wrote it in Greek, it was one long sentence—202 words! This passage is breathtaking not only in its length but also in its glorious truth.

Underline each word or phrase describing God's choice, will, or timing. Circle each mention of "in Christ," "in him," or a similar idea.

Blessed is the God and Father of our Lord Jesus Christ, who has blessed us with every spiritual blessing in the heavens in Christ. For he chose us in him, before the foundation of the world, to be holy and blameless in love before him. He predestined us to be adopted as sons through Jesus Christ for himself, according to the good pleasure of his will, to the praise of his glorious grace that he lavished on us in the Beloved One. In him we have redemption through his blood, the forgiveness of our trespasses, according to the riches of his grace that he richly poured out on us with all wisdom and understanding. He made known to us the mystery of his will, according to his good pleasure that he purposed in Christ as a plan for the right time—to bring everything together in Christ, both things in heaven and things on earth in him. In him we have also received an inheritance, because we were predestined according to the plan of the one who works out everything in agreement with the purpose of his will, so that we who had already put our hope in Christ might bring praise to his glory. In him you also were sealed with the promised Holy Spirit when you heard the word of truth, the gospel of your salvation, and when you believed. The Holy Spirit is the down payment of our inheritance, until the redemption of the possession, to the praise of his glory.
EPHESIANS 1:3-14

What confidence should it give you to realize that Christ specifically chose you to love, know, and save?

What's one key truth from the previous passage that you need to take to heart and meditate on today?

You could read that sentence over and over again for the rest of eternity, and it would never grow old. It would only grow more amazing. Thank God for His unbelievably gracious love for you. Before you did a single thing to prove yourself worthy or unworthy of His favor, He chose you.

Day 2
I AM NO LONGER CONDEMNED

Highlight each description of your new identity in the following verses.

*You are a chosen race, a royal priesthood, a holy nation,
a people for his possession, so that you may proclaim the praises
of the one who called you out of darkness into his marvelous light.
Once you were not a people, but now you are God's people;
you had not received mercy, but now you have received mercy.*
1 PETER 2:9-10

Race. Priesthood. Nation. People. Do you remember the immediate effect of sin for Adam and Eve? Guilt. Shame. Hiding. Self-preservation. Broken fellowship. Consequences. Your new identity in Christ is one in which fellowship has been restored. You're set free from the curse of sin's self-centered desires.

Chosen. Royal. Holy. His possession. Called out. Received mercy. You were called "out of darkness into his marvelous light" (v. 9). You're no longer condemned; you're chosen by grace.

While every one of those descriptions of your new identity is true, which is the most meaningful to you right now? Why?

Whom do you know who may have a relationship with Jesus but is living with a burden of defeat, guilt, shame, or loneliness? How can you remind them that Christ has called them out of darkness and into freedom and fellowship?

Paul wrote one of the most liberating sentences in human history. He was able to write it because he knew the life-changing grace found in Christ. The gospel of Jesus transformed a persecutor of Christ into a proclaimer of grace. Romans 8, one of the most glorious chapters in all of Scripture, begins this way:

*There is now no condemnation for those in Christ Jesus,
because the law of the Spirit of life in Christ Jesus
has set you free from the law of sin and death.*
ROMANS 8:1-2

Circle "no condemnation" and "set you free." Underline "in Christ Jesus."

Sin brings death and condemnation before God. The seeming good life apart from Christ is slavery to your own desires. Because of Jesus you're free from condemnation. You're free from your own empty pursuits. Jesus has made you truly alive. Sin no longer has any claim on you. Where there once was condemnation, you have new life. Jesus has set you free. Where there once was darkness, there's now marvelous light. Live in that freedom. Proclaim this good news to everyone around you. Invite others to join you in freedom and in fellowship.

Though we want to live in freedom, we sometimes still feel condemned even when God says we aren't. How should we respond in those moments?

Why should we refuse to let our feelings be the ultimate source of truth?

God is the One with the authority to declare who we are. He says we're not condemned even when we feel that we are. God has full authority as Creator, Savior, and Judge to give us our identity independent of our feelings and circumstances:

If the Son makes you free, you will be free indeed.
JOHN 8:36, NASB

Conclude your personal study by proclaiming the praises of your Savior. Pray that the Holy Spirit will constantly remind you of your true and total freedom in Christ. Also pray for discernment and boldness to share the good news of freedom with people around you.

Day 3
I AM A SON

One of the most common ways Jesus referred to God was Father. This title was significant in clarifying Jesus' unique identity as the Son of God. What's even more amazing is that Jesus not only spoke of God as His Father but also taught His disciples to do the same:

> *You should pray like this:*
> *Our Father in heaven,*
> *your name be honored as holy.*
> *Your kingdom come.*
> *Your will be done*
> *on earth as it is in heaven.*
> *Give us today our daily bread.*
> *And forgive us our debts,*
> *as we also have forgiven our debtors.*
> *And do not bring us into temptation,*
> *but deliver us from the evil one.*
> MATTHEW 6:9-13

In what has come to be known as the Model Prayer or the Lord's Prayer, Jesus provided a picture of life—a family portrait. Relationship. Honor. Holiness. Trust. Obedience. Provision. Blessing. Forgiveness. Guidance. Protection. These characteristics are vital parts of your new identity in Christ. Your Heavenly Father desires to relate to you in these ways. No matter what your earthly experiences have been with family—good or bad—your Heavenly Father is good, and so is life in His family.

The phrase "born again" describes a person's new identity through faith in Christ and his or her new relationship with God, our Heavenly Father. Jesus' conversation with Nicodemus, a religious leader who came to visit him one night in the darkness (remember that the author, John, loved the theme of darkness and light), centered on the idea of being born again. At the moment Nicodemus just couldn't wrap his mind around it all:

> *Jesus answered, "Truly I tell you, unless someone is born of water*
> *and the Spirit, he cannot enter the kingdom of God. Whatever is born*
> *of the flesh is flesh, and whatever is born of the Spirit is spirit.*
> *Do not be amazed that I told you that you must be born again."*
> JOHN 3:5-7

John clearly stated that all who believe in Jesus are born again as children of God:

> *To all who did receive him, he gave them the right to be children of*
> *God, to those who believe in his name, who were born, not of natural*
> *descent, or of the will of the flesh, or of the will of man, but of God.*
> JOHN 1:12-13

According to these verses, how do we become children of God?

When you're born again, you become a child of God and a coheir with Christ. Everything that belongs to Him now belongs to you too. This is why the Bible often says you're a son, whether you're a male or a female. In biblical times, in both the Old and the New Testaments, sons received the family inheritance. Your Heavenly Father has leveled the playing field in Christ. No matter what your background was, who your parents were, or what you've done, when you're born again, you're a son of God—a coheir in the kingdom of God.

No matter what kind of relationship you have with your earthly father, you have a perfect Heavenly Father. How should being a child of God influence the way you view and think about yourself?

Record the names of family members, either thanking God that they've already believed in Jesus or asking God to call them out of darkness so that they can be born again through faith in God's only Son and can receive eternal life with Him.

Day 4
I AM HIS WORKMANSHIP

You don't work *for* God's favor; you work *from* God's favor. What does this statement mean? It means you don't have to earn God's approval and affection. Your Heavenly Father fully and perfectly delights in you, His child.

Do you remember God's repeated assessment after days 3–5 of creation in Genesis 1?

It was _____.

On day 6, however, God created man and woman in His own image, blessed them, and gave them work to do. What was his conclusion? It was _____ _____ indeed.

God has created you to do His work. This was God's great design for human life since the beginning, before sin twisted the nature of work into something painful and difficult. Originally, human work was a matter of joining God's work to bring order and purpose to the world. The first man and woman were helpers together in their God-given responsibilities of naming animals; tending the garden; ruling over and subduing creation; and, of course, being fruitful and multiplying, filling the earth with image bearers of the Creator.

All the man and the woman had to do was to trust and obey their Creator, and they would experience the incomparable satisfaction of fulfilling their unique purpose according to their design. The work they were given wasn't to earn the approval of their Creator or to fix what was lacking and incomplete. He didn't need their help. He didn't need their performance. He blessed them with their work. Their work was an expression of who they were. Their identity came with a purpose: to do the work God had prepared for them. And it was very good.

Honestly, which choice best fits your view of work?
☐ **Evil: I hate it.**
☐ **A necessary evil: It is what it is.**
☐ **Blessing: I love it.**

God, who is rich in mercy, because of his great love that he had for us, made us alive with Christ even though we were dead in trespasses. You are saved by grace! He also raised us up with him and seated us with him in the heavens in Christ Jesus, so that in the coming ages he might display the immeasurable riches of his grace through his kindness to us in Christ Jesus. For you are saved by grace through faith, and this is not from yourselves; it is God's gift— not from works, so that no one can boast. For we are his workmanship, created in Christ Jesus for good works, which God prepared ahead of time for us to do.
EPHESIANS 2:4-10

God made you His child and a coheir with Christ. He made you for good works. He made you His workmanship. The word that's translated as "workmanship" in verse 10 is the Greek word *poiema*. You may recognize its similarity to the English word *poem*. That's exactly what Paul meant when he wrote this letter to the churches in the city of Ephesus. You're God's poem. His beautiful and thoughtful self-expression. His masterpiece. He made you from an overflow of His creative joy as His workmanship. You bear His unique stamp and signature. Just as a poem points back to its author, we point back to ours. Our work is to make Jesus known. Each of us makes Jesus known in distinct ways, using our gifts and callings to complete the good works God has prepared for us to walk in.

How does being God's workmanship—His masterful creation— shape the way you view yourself?

What gifts has God given you to contribute to His work in the world? How do your gifts shape the way you view the work He has given you to do?

Thank God that no matter what your vocation may be, He has given you good work to do. Pray for the motivation and perspective to do it wholeheartedly as His image bearer:

Whether you eat or drink, or whatever you do, do everything for the glory of God.
1 CORINTHIANS 10:31

Day 5
TAKE FIVE: IDENTITY

Use the space below to record five main takeaways God taught you through the group session and personal studies this week. You may want to choose one truth from each day, or certain days may have been especially meaningful to you.

1.

2.

3.

4.

5.

In an Old Testament prophecy found in Isaiah 49, the Lord declared His love for His chosen people, Israel. After He reminded them of their identity in Him, He reminded them of His purpose for their lives. God declared that He would work not only in them but also through them so that the whole world would see His glory and greatness. He then used a vivid image to express the unchanging nature of their identity and purpose:

> *Look, I have inscribed you on the palms of my hands.*
> ISAIAH 49:16

We are always before God. We are on His hands and in His heart.

With this mental picture of your new identity in mind, read the five ideas you wrote on the previous page. Then read the following passage.

> *How happy is the one who does not*
> *walk in the advice of the wicked*
> *or stand in the pathway with sinners*
> *or sit in the company of mockers!*
> *Instead, his delight is in the LORD's instruction,*
> *and he meditates on it day and night.*
> *He is like a tree planted beside flowing streams*
> *that bears its fruit in its season*
> *and whose leaf does not wither.*
> *Whatever he does prospers.*
> PSALM 1:1-3

Read Psalm 1 in your Bible. Let it guide a time of prayerful reflection.

Week 5

WHAT WE HAVE IN CHRIST

Start

We'll start by reviewing what we learned in the previous week's personal studies. Refer to your notes in week 4, especially day 5, when answering these questions with the group.

What new truth did you learn, or what stood out to you this week?

Why is knowing that God chose you vital to a healthy view of your life (day 1)?

What was the most significant truth you learned as you reflected on condemnation and freedom (day 2)?

How does the biblical concept of workmanship express itself in our lives (day 4)?

Our new identity comes with a rich inheritance. This week we'll focus on what we've received in Christ.

After praying, watch the video teaching.

Watch

Use this section to take notes as you watch video session 5.

God the Father has had a will and a plan from before the world began, and He's carrying out that plan to adopt us and to give us an inheritance.

Because Jesus is our Lord, we are joint heirs with Christ. That means what He has, we have in Him.

Our Inheritance in Christ

1. Salvation and forgiveness
2. Eternal life
3. A Heavenly Father
4. Blessings
5. A spiritual family
6. A home in heaven
7. A hope in this life

Our inheritance is imperishable, undefiled, and unfading.

We have hope of eternal life that we can look forward to because of our relationship with God through Jesus.

The hope we have in Jesus is a sure hope, based on His promises.

Discuss

After viewing the video, discuss the following questions with your group.

What points in the video were most significant for you?

What are the greatest gifts and guarantees we've received in Christ? Before watching the video, would you have answered the question differently?

Why is hope so important to our lives? How is hope related to identity? What differences between worldly hope and Christian hope were identified on the video?

How would you explain our hope for each of the grand finales in Christ?
• The return of Christ
• Salvation
• Transformation
• Judgment
• Heaven

On a scale of 1 to 10, with 1 being terrified and 10 being terrifically excited, how do you feel about life beyond death? Does your life match what you say you believe about eternal hope in Christ?

Read Ephesians 1:13-23 and Revelation 21:1-8; 22:1-5.

What thoughts and feelings did you experience while reading those Scriptures? What promises gave you the most hope? Why do you think those promises were especially meaningful?

In what ways has this session been encouraging, convicting, or well timed?

After discussion, close the session with prayer.

Day 1
LOVE

Have you ever been watching a movie or listening to a song and noticed something that had never stood out to you before? Maybe knowing the end of the story helped you pick up on clues earlier. Perhaps wearing headphones brought clarity to a subtle detail in the background that you never noticed while that same track was on repeat during your daily commute. And speaking of commuting, have you ever walked or driven past the same places day after day and discovered a new spot—a coffee shop, a park, a side street with public art—only to learn later that it had been there all along?

Before turning the corner into the second half of Ephesians, which addresses the practical implications of living out your new identity in Christ, we'll spend one more week examining some key phrases about your identity. You don't want to miss these hidden gems simply because you've been focusing on other signs along the way. At the beginning of Ephesians we see that from eternity past, we've been chosen by God:

> *[God] chose us in him, before the foundation of the world,*
> *to be holy and blameless in love before him.*
> EPHESIANS 1:4

What does it mean to you to know that you've been chosen from God before you even existed?

Don't rush past that thought as ordinary or familiar. God not only chose you. God not only loves you. God chose to love you. God wasn't obligated to love you or to save you. But by His good will it pleased Him not only to create you and redeem you but also to pursue a personal relationship with you. He's not only your Creator. He's not only your Savior. He's not only your Lord. He's your Heavenly Father too. He's all of these. He has chosen to love you.

What keeps you from experiencing the fullness of God's love for you? Do you think you could do something or could have done something to make God love you less or not at all?

Though our love may wane and we may not feel loved, the truth is that nothing can ever keep God from loving you. His affection for you is fixed:

> *Who can separate us from the love of Christ? Can affliction or distress or*
> *persecution or famine or nakedness or danger or sword? As it is written:*
> *Because of you*
> *we are being put to death all day long;*
> *we are counted as sheep to be slaughtered.*
> *No, in all these things we are more than conquerors through him*
> *who loved us. For I am persuaded that neither death nor life, nor*
> *angels nor rulers, nor things present nor things to come, nor powers,*
> *nor height nor depth, nor any other created thing will be able to*
> *separate us from the love of God that is in Christ Jesus our Lord.*
> ROMANS 8:35-39

How does this truth provide comfort? How does it provide courage?

What would change if you truly believed God loves you?

In both of the previous Scriptures, Paul used the Greek word *agape* to express the love of Christ for us. *Agape* was a favorite word in the writings of Paul, John, and Peter. This kind of love is more than affection or even loyalty. It's a proactive, unconditional benevolence. *Agape* love seeks to provide what's best for someone, regardless of cost or the person's worthiness.

There are too many Scriptures even to scratch the surface about God's inexhaustible, all-consuming, and life-giving love. For now use the following verse to prayerfully reflect on God's love for you. Highlight key words.

> *The LORD your God is among you,*
> *a warrior who saves.*
> *He will rejoice over you with gladness.*
> *He will be quiet in his love.*
> *He will delight in you with singing.*
> ZEPHANIAH 3:17

Day 2
REDEMPTION/
FORGIVENESS

I never stop giving thanks for you as I remember you in my prayers.
I pray that the God of our Lord Jesus Christ, the glorious Father, would
give you the Spirit of wisdom and revelation in the knowledge of him.
EPHESIANS 1:16-17

Paul often stopped to pray or to share what he was praying for the recipients of his letters. In this particular prayer, one that includes all three Persons of the Trinity—Father, Son, and Holy Spirit—Paul asked God to give the Ephesian believers wisdom, revelation, and knowledge.

Paul's practice is a great habit to develop in your life. Pray whenever the Spirit brings someone to mind or when you recognize beauty or needs around you. Let people know you're praying for them and what you're praying on their behalf. In doing so, you can bring a perfectly timed word of encouragement, hope, or conviction to their lives.

Who or what comes to mind? Take a moment to pray for anyone the Lord brings to mind. Praise God, make requests, or confess any sin He places on your heart.

When Paul stopped to record the previous prayers, he was describing the overwhelming reality of the Ephesians' new identity in Christ. Recall that verses 3-13 leading up to these prayers were one epic sentence in the original Greek language. It's almost as if Paul was in such awe of the glorious truth that he had written on parchment that he paused for a personal praise break. He also stopped to express praise in Romans 11:33-36 and Ephesians 3:14-21.

In each of those prayerful praise breaks, Paul had been proclaiming the mystery of God in choosing to love people and in creating a new family from sinners who were saved by His grace through their faith in Jesus. Only in Christ were salvation, the forgiveness of sin, and a new heart made possible. Look back at the sentences describing this new reality:

In him [Jesus] we have redemption through his blood, the forgiveness of our
trespasses, according to the riches of his grace that he richly poured out on
us with all wisdom and understanding. He made known to us the mystery
of his will, according to his good pleasure that he purposed in Christ.
EPHESIANS 1:7-9

An entire culture is devoted to leveraging your insecurity, guilt, shame, and fear
through advertising, social media, and countless images and experiences blatantly or
subtly portrayed through media and entertainment. A deafening chorus of "You're
not good enough" rings in your ears and parades before your eyes daily. That's why
yesterday's proclamation that nothing and no one can separate you from the love of
Christ is essential. That's the instinctive reflex with which you need to retrain your
heart when you're attacked with lies of guilt and emptiness. God chose to purchase
your freedom, and He doesn't have buyer's remorse. He chose to redeem you. You're
eternally forgiven by the riches of Jesus' precious blood.

Fill in the blanks with your name.

As high as the heavens are above the earth,
so great is his faithful love
toward _____.
As far as the east is from the west,
so far has he removed … transgressions from _____.
As a father has compassion on his children,
so the LORD *has compassion on _____*
For he knows what _____ [is] made of,
remembering that _____ [is] dust.
PSALM 103:11-14

Why should we regularly reflect on these truths?

Read Psalm 103 as a personal prayer to conclude your study today. Confess any sin
that lingers in your heart and mind, causing guilt and shame to cloud your vision.
Ask for eyes to see yourself as God sees you—fully forgiven and loved. Ask for ears
to hear what He declares to be true about you in His Word.

Day 3
ACCESS

The love and forgiveness you have in Christ are so much more than not getting into trouble. The Christian life is greater than going to heaven when you die, as great as that prospect is. The gospel isn't just a get-out-of-jail-free card or a mask you can put on so that when God looks at you, He sees Jesus. Being forgiven isn't merely the erasure of your debt to sin. It's an invitation into a close personal relationship with your Redeemer:

Through him [Jesus] we both have access in one Spirit to the Father.
EPHESIANS 2:18

Don't let your heart be troubled. Believe in God; believe also
in me. In my Father's house are many rooms; if not, I would
have told you. I am going away to prepare a place for you.
If I go away and prepare a place for you, I will come again
and take you to myself, so that where I am you may be also.
JOHN 14:1-3

You've received the house key. Too many Christians would say that God loves them and that they've been forgiven through faith in the gospel of Jesus' death and resurrection, but they live as if God doesn't like them or doesn't want to be around them. They may believe that they'll go to heaven when they die but that their room will be in the old part of town that God doesn't visit or pass through.

However, in Christ you have every benefit as a member of God's household. He longs for you to be an active, integral part of His family. He's your *Abba,* an Aramaic word meaning "Daddy." Being the son or the daughter of a perfect Abba means you have access to a devoted, loving Father.

> **Read Romans 8:14-16. What does the name Abba reveal about the relationship that God desires and that the Holy Spirit makes possible?**

> **Read Romans 8:26-27. How does the Holy Spirit help you relate to your Heavenly Father?**

> **Read Matthew 7:7-11. What did Jesus reveal about prayer?**

Beyond being redeemed, you have a good God who's near and who hears your prayers. Even when you don't quite know what to say in prayer, He knows your heart and what you need. He desires conversation. He invites you into His presence. The way Jesus talked about God as His Father and ours made some people uncomfortable enough. What was totally shocking at the time was taking that image of access to God and applying it to the temple:

> *Now in Christ Jesus, you who were far away*
> *have been brought near by the blood of Christ.*
> EPHESIANS 2:13

> *Since we have a great high priest who has passed through the heavens—*
> *Jesus the Son of God—let us hold fast to our confession. For we do not*
> *have a high priest who is unable to sympathize with our weaknesses,*
> *but one who has been tempted in every way as we are, yet without sin.*
> *Therefore, let us approach the throne of grace with boldness, so that*
> *we may receive mercy and find grace to help us in time of need.*
> HEBREWS 4:14-16

When Jesus died on the cross, the temple curtain was torn from top to bottom, as if God Himself had grasped it and ripped it apart (see Matt. 27:51). Jesus' redemptive work was finished. His people were no longer separated from His holy presence and no longer needed priests and sacrifices to intercede on their behalf. Christ knows what you're going through. No human thought, feeling, or experience is trivial or beneath Him. He invites you to come talk to Him—to come boldly to His throne.

God has thrown the door wide open and invited you to come boldly into His presence, taking a seat and making yourself at home. He's your Abba. Christ has made you part of the family and has given you the house key.

What concerns do you need to take to God with boldness and faith today?

Praise God that not just in heaven but even now you have twenty-four-hour access to Him through prayer. Thank Him for being with you always.

Day 4
GOOD WORKS TO WALK IN

We are His workmanship, created in Christ Jesus for good works,
which God prepared beforehand so that we would walk in them.
EPHESIANS 2:10, NASB

The first part of this verse could feel like an overwhelming burden without the second part. Who could ever live up to the expectation of being God's masterpiece? Everybody knows we all fall short of the glory of God, right (see Rom. 3:23)? Being His workmanship sounds great, like a poster to hang or a quotation to share. But it might not feel very true.

The good works we're supposed to do often feel like cross-country skiing. You put snow skis on your feet, grip ski poles in your hands, and start pushing your way across snowy terrain. Before you were in Christ, this was a picture of your life. You worked your way along, pushing and pulling and trying to build momentum to keep you moving toward your goal. Maybe you didn't even have a goal in sight; you just knew you were supposed to keep moving.

Even as a Christian, you may still feel this way at times. Even though there's a fairly clear path for you and you know where you'll end up, you're still trekking along in your own strength and occasionally feel worn-out from the journey.

Paul wasn't describing heroic self-effort but the completed work of Christ on our behalf. Our responsibility as the people of God is to move freely in His strength and power. Rather than cross-country skiing, the picture is more like a slalom. You still put on skis and grasp poles, but rather than continually propelling you along, the poles help you keep your balance as you rush downhill in the power of gravity. It still takes practice and skill, and you sometimes fall, but ultimately you learn to move in a power that isn't your own. You're stepping into it, and it's moving you forward. You either try to resist and redirect, or you cooperate with that power and become better and better at following the path that's been marked out by the one who designed the course.

When you think about doing good works for God, do you feel a sense of obligation and burden or joy and love? Explain.

How does knowing that God prepared works for you beforehand free you to obey with hope and expectation?

How have you notice God working in the world around you? How can you join the work God is already doing?

The pressure is off to do the right thing in your own power and wisdom. Just lean in and trust God. It's not up to you to determine the results. We find where God is already up to something and get involved by loving and serving others. Obey Him, follow His lead, and enjoy the ride. When you fall down, get back up and keep going. Jesus described a life walking in His work this way:

> *Come to me, all of you who are weary and burdened, and I will give you rest. Take up my yoke and learn from me, because I am lowly and humble in heart, and you will find rest for your souls. For my yoke is easy and my burden is light.*
> MATTHEW 11:28-30

Jesus invites you not to do work for Him but rather with Him. The religious leaders of Jesus' day were piling up rule on rule on rule, creating an impossible weight for people to carry. Following God had become no more than a list of do's and don'ts.

A yoke is what an ox or a donkey would wear around its neck to shoulder a heavy load. Jesus promised that the work He had prepared for us will bring rest and peace. The only way this is possible is because He carries the weight with us. We don't work in our own strength but in His. The burden has been laid on Him, and we share in the benefit.

In what ways do you need to trust God more fully, stop working for favor, and start enjoying the grace you've received? How could this approach transform the work you do for Jesus?

Conclude your personal study by asking the Holy Spirit to give you discernment to recognize the ways He's at work and boldness to join in that work.

Day 5
TAKE FIVE: BLESSINGS

Use the space below to record five main takeaways God taught you through the group session and personal studies this week. You may want to choose one truth from each day, or certain days may have been especially meaningful to you.

1.

2.

3.

4.

5.

All four Gospels include an emotional account of a woman at the feet of Jesus (see Matt. 26:6-13; Mark 14:3-9; Luke 7:36-50; John 12:1-8). Unlike the woman caught in adultery, who was dragged into the street, this woman entered a home where Jesus was seated at the table. While some onlookers scoffed in arrogance, this woman knelt in humility, pouring out her heart with tears and perfumed oil and wiping the Lord's feet with her hair.

Nothing was more precious to the woman than showing honor to the King of grace. Not her dignity. Not her reputation. Not her appearance. Not her possessions—even one that was worth a full year's income. This extravagant display was unthinkable for most people in the room. They couldn't believe Jesus would let the woman touch Him or could be pleased by such a wasteful use of resources, but Jesus welcomed her into His presence and blessed her act of love. He even modeled similar behavior for His disciples, washing their feet the night He was betrayed.

Picture yourself on hands and knees, overflowing with gratitude for the gracious blessings that are yours in Christ. Consider all He has given you and what you wouldn't give or do for the Lord. Then read the following passage.

The LORD is my shepherd;
I have what I need.
He lets me lie down in green pastures;
he leads me beside quiet waters.
He renews my life;
he leads me along the right paths
for his name's sake.
Even when I go through the darkest valley,
I fear no danger,
for you are with me;
your rod and your staff—they comfort me.
PSALM 23:1-4

Read Psalm 23 in your Bible. Let it guide a time of prayerful reflection.

LIVING OUT OUR IDENTITY

Start

We'll start by reviewing what we learned in the previous week's personal studies. Refer to your notes in week 5, especially day 5, when answering these questions with the group.

What stood out to you most about God's love (day 1)?

How does access to God result from His love and forgiveness (day 3)?

How does access to God empower us to work with Him (day 4)?

Does anybody have a quick story to share about walking in the opportunities God provided this week to join Him in His work?

Now that we know what it means to have an identity in Christ, we need to learn how that identity becomes a part of who we are. Living out our identity includes throwing off our former selves and putting on our new selves. The last three chapters of Ephesians repeatedly highlight ways God changes our words, our thinking, our attitudes, our habits, and our relationships.

After praying, watch the video teaching.

Watch

Use this section to take notes as you watch video session 6.

When you're at an extreme—you think too much of yourself or you don't think enough of yourself—usually you're not abiding in the identify God has for you.

Put Off	*Put On*
Lying	Truth
Stealing	Working and sharing
Unwholesome talk	Blessing
Bitterness, anger	Kind, tenderhearted
Immorality, unwholesome talk	Giving thanks
Darkness	Light: goodness, righteousness, truth
Foolishness	God's will
Drunkenness	The filling of the Spirit

We're now beloved children. We need to walk in love toward other people.

Let your life be transformed by who you are and what you have in Christ.

Discuss

—————

After viewing the video, discuss the following questions with your group.

What points in the video were most significant for you?

Why did we spend more than half of this study emphasizing who we are before addressing what we can and should do as followers of Christ?

What examples can you recall in Scripture when commands not to do something are related to something better that God desires for us? How does this reality change your perspective on obedience?

Read Ephesians 4:17-32. What negative things are we told to put off or avoid? What better things are we told to put on or do instead?

Which of the things on this list do we tend to justify? Which do we judge more harshly? Why do we differentiate when God says to put it all away?

In what ways have you experienced God's grace and the power of the Holy Spirit in taking off the old self and putting on the new self?

How is God working in your relationships with family members? At work? In your community? In your church?

In what areas of your life are you failing to live "worthy of the calling you have received" (Eph. 4:1) in Christ? How can we pray for one another?

In what ways has this session been encouraging, convicting, or well timed?

After discussion, close the session prayer.

Day 1
RENEW YOUR MIND

*I have been crucified with Christ, and I no longer live, but Christ
lives in me. The life I now live in the body, I live by faith in
the Son of God, who loved me and gave himself for me.*
GALATIANS 2:20

How would you describe living by faith in the Son of God?

Last week you studied the reality of what it means to walk in the good works God
prepared for you. Moving in the strength and power of the Lord doesn't mean
passively doing nothing. It means that He carries the load. He's responsible for the
outcome. How then do you stay in step with Him? If you have to actively partici-
pate by following Christ and wearing His yoke, how do you know which way to go
and which step to take?

*The LORD directs the steps of the godly.
He delights in every detail of their lives.*
PSALM 37:23, NLT

In what parts of your life do you act as if God doesn't care about them?

**How does the previous verse change the intentionality with which you view
those parts of your life and your decision whether to do those things in the
future?**

Every detail of your life forms a rhythm. Your routines and experiences become
habits that are like songs stuck in your head. You repeat them over and over without
thinking much about them. To live out your new identity, you need a new pattern
of thinking:

Brothers and sisters, in view of the mercies of God, I urge you to present your bodies as a living sacrifice, holy and pleasing to God; this is your true worship. Do not be conformed to this age, but be transformed by the renewing of your mind, so that you may discern what is the good, pleasing, and perfect will of God.
ROMANS 12:1-2

What did Paul say is the motivation for a new way of living (see v. 1)?

What did Paul mean by the phrase "your true worship" (v. 1)?

Paul said God's character and activity should motivate you to live differently than the world around you. Specifically, His mercy—choosing to forgive your sin and make you part of His holy family—should transform the desires of your heart so that you want to please God. When you have the desire to please Him, everything in your life becomes an act of worship. Whether on weekdays or weekends, no matter where you are or what you're doing, your worship isn't limited to singing songs or attending activities at a set time or place. Everything is worship. Technically, this was always true; everything has always been an act of worship. The problem was that your worship was self-centered. In Christ your worship is now a matter of dying to yourself and pleasing God rather than following your own heart.

Notice that Paul said you can know God's will. God isn't trying to hide His will from you. It isn't a mystery you have to solve by discerning random signs and clues. God has given you His Spirit; His Word; and His people, the church. You'll look more closely at each of those resources in coming days, but for now notice one important detail. Paul instructed brothers and sisters in Christ to present their bodies (plural) as a living sacrifice (singular). Your identity isn't purely individual. In Christ you're now part of His body, the church.

Conclude this lesson by reading Ephesians 4:1-16 and by identifying ways Paul clarified the idea of renewing your mind in order to be a living sacrifice.

Day 2
CHANGE YOUR CLOTHES

When you renew your mind and live as part of Christ's body, it's essential that you continue to wake up and live out this reality day after day, week after week, year after year. And what's a mandatory step in any morning routine? Clothes.

Take off your former way of life, the old self that is corrupted by deceitful desires, ... be renewed in the spirit of your minds, and ... put on the new self, the one created according to God's likeness in righteousness and purity of the truth.
EPHESIANS 4:22-24

"Take off" (v. 22) and "put on" (v. 24) are both commands to Christians. What do these commands teach you about living out your new identity?

Paul didn't mean you need to be born again every morning. You don't need to be resaved every time you sin. Remember, you'll fall. Get back up again. You're forgiven. Paul meant submitting your body "as a living sacrifice, holy and pleasing to God" (Rom. 12:1), is an ongoing process. You never outgrow the need to renew your mind and to put on the new self. Resisting sin is an active process.

Read Colossians 3:5-10. What strikes you most about these verses?

What parts of your old self need to be thrown out?

Sexual immorality   *Impurity*   *Lust*

Evil desire   *Greed (idolatry)*   *Anger*

Wrath   *Malice*   *Slander*

Filthy language   *Lying*

Read Colossians 3:12-15. What strikes you most about these verses?

What parts of your new self need to be put on?

Compassion   *Kindness*   *Humility*

Gentleness   *Patience*   *Forgiveness*   *Love*

Unity   *Peace*   *Thankfulness*

Notice that Paul said to take off, put to death, and put away the old self. Too often the excuse "Nobody is perfect" translates into a desire to hang on to our dirty laundry. We may take off most of the old self for a while, but we leave it lying around so that we can put it back on when we're under stress. We're used to the old. It's comfortable. It's familiar. But the fact is, it stinks of death.

We also need to recognize that it doesn't do any good to try putting new clothes over old ones. We can't simply cover up or hide the old self under outward appearance. That's the kind of hypocrisy that Jesus condemned:

> *Woe to you, scribes and Pharisees, hypocrites! You are like whitewashed tombs,*
> *which appear beautiful on the outside, but inside are full of the bones of the*
> *dead and every kind of impurity. In the same way, on the outside you seem*
> *righteous to people, but inside you are full of hypocrisy and lawlessness.*
> MATTHEW 23:27-28

If there are areas of your life that stink of hypocrisy, confess those now, taking off the character and behavior of your old self and surrendering them to Christ. You're not fooling anyone with your religious appearance except maybe yourself. It's nothing but fig leaves. Let God wrap you in His infinite love and the new self that transforms you from the inside out:

> *I pray that you, being rooted and firmly established in love, may be*
> *able to comprehend with all the saints what is the length and width,*
> *height and depth of God's love, and to know Christ's love that surpasses*
> *knowledge, so that you may be filled with all the fullness of God.*
> EPHESIANS 3:17-19

Day 3
WATCH YOUR MOUTH

Yesterday Jesus had strong words for the religious hypocrisy of draping a clean appearance over lifeless bones. The difference between man-made religion and a new identity in Christ is that religious effort and acceptable morality deal only with the facade of our lives. The new self is transformed from the inside out. Jesus elaborated on that idea throughout the Gospels, using the image of fruit:

> *A good tree doesn't produce bad fruit; on the other hand, a bad tree doesn't produce good fruit. For each tree is known by its own fruit. Figs aren't gathered from thornbushes, or grapes picked from a bramble bush. A good person produces good out of the good stored up in his heart. An evil person produces evil out of the evil stored up in his heart, for his mouth speaks from the overflow of the heart.*
> LUKE 6:43-45

What does Jesus' teaching reveal about your speech?

How is Jesus' teaching contrary to popular opinion about words?

What comes out of us reveals what's inside us. This is true of actions in general. That's why the first portion of this study focused on your identity. Your actions reveal the nature of your heart. Outward religion and moral behavior modification can never change a person's nature. Read another of Paul's spontaneous prayers:

> *I pray that he [God] may grant you, according to the riches of his glory, to be strengthened with power in your inner being through his Spirit, and that Christ may dwell in your hearts through faith. I pray that you, being rooted and firmly established in love ...*
> EPHESIANS 3:16-17

Good fruit needs good roots. What did Paul say is inside you?

*Let the word of Christ dwell richly among you, in all wisdom
teaching and admonishing one another through psalms, hymns,
and spiritual songs, singing to God with gratitude in your hearts.
And whatever you do, in word or in deed, do everything in the name
of the Lord Jesus, giving thanks to God the Father through him.*
COLOSSIANS 3:16-17

**What must you put into your heart and mind in order for words of this
nature to come out of you?**

It's imperative that you, as a new creation in Christ, continually take off and set
aside the old self while putting on the new self, renewing your mind in Christ
Jesus and strengthening your inner being. When you're filled to all the fullness of
God, the love of Christ will spill out in your words. Planting seeds of truth through
Scripture and spiritual songs will take root and bear fruit. What you read, listen to,
and watch are all seeds that will produce fruit.

Read Philippians 2:14-16. What did Paul warn against and why?

Read Ephesians 4:25-32. Make a list of the bad fruit and good fruit.

Bad Fruit	**Good Fruit**

Conclude your personal study by prayerfully reflecting on what the fruit of your lips
reveals about the condition of your heart. Commit to filling your heart and mind
with the Word of God, which will grow and produce good fruit:

*Whatever is true, whatever is honorable, whatever is just, whatever is
pure, whatever is lovely, whatever is commendable—if there is any moral
excellence and if there is anything praiseworthy—dwell on these things.*
PHILIPPIANS 4:8

Day 4
KNOW WHOM YOU BELONG TO

It's easy to look at men like Paul and be amazed by his ability to accomplish so much for the kingdom of God. Perhaps you see the men and women in the Bible as superheroes of the faith. On the other hand, it can be tempting to discount their faith, thinking that if Jesus had miraculously shown up in your life, you'd live more boldly too. But remember, the overwhelming majority of the people during Jesus' time didn't believe in Him. In fact, they even had Jesus crucified as a blasphemous teacher who was trying to incite a rebellion.

This perspective again points to the reality that a heart change has to take place. We have to experience a radical transformation of identity and allegiance. Until we're living as a part of God's kingdom with an understanding of what it means to be His image bearer, we'll naturally do anything we need to do for comfort, gain, and self-preservation.

Read Philippians 4:11-13. What did Paul reveal as his great secret?

Do biblical stories of men and women inspire you, intimidate you, or both? When reading them, do you feel your faith growing or a sense of failure? Explain your answer.

We often treat the men and women of the Bible as superhuman giants of faith. In reality, they were just normal men and women who knew they belonged to God. Paul described this commitment in his second letter to Timothy:

Don't be ashamed of the testimony about our Lord, or of me his prisoner. Instead, share in suffering for the gospel, relying on the power of God. He has saved us and called us with a holy calling, not according to our works, but according to his own purpose and grace, which was given to us in Christ Jesus before time began.
2 TIMOTHY 1:8-9

How does that reminder from 2 Timothy help frame your sense of worth and calling?

Paul continued his instruction to Timothy, his young protégé, by turning any attention away from personal accomplishments, past or present, and by fixing attention purely on what the Savior had done. From that victory, unshakable confidence fueled their work to proclaim the gospel—the good news that life and salvation aren't about us but about Jesus. Paul was able to lead, rejoice, suffer, and continue in faith because he knew Jesus and believed Jesus would always be with Him:

> *This has now been made evident through the appearing of our Savior Christ Jesus, who has abolished death and has brought life and immortality to light through the gospel. For this gospel I was appointed a herald, apostle, and teacher, and that is why I suffer these things. But I am not ashamed, because I know whom I have believed and am persuaded that he is able to guard what has been entrusted to me until that day.*
> 2 TIMOTHY 1:10-12

What should be different about your life because you understand that Jesus knows you and loves you?

Whom do you know who's finding worth in something else and needs to hear, "Jesus loves you"? When will you tell them?

Conclude your study today by praying that God will help you grow increasingly confident, not in yourself but in knowing the One whom you've believed. Pray that you'll be persuaded—convinced—that He's able to do all things and that therefore, in faith, you have nothing to fear:

> *I can do all things through Him who strengthens me.*
> PHILIPPIANS 4:13, NASB

Day 5
TAKE FIVE: ACTION

Use the space below to record five main takeaways God taught you through the group session and personal studies this week. You may want to choose one truth from each day, or certain days may have been especially meaningful to you.

1.

2.

3.

4.

5.

Shortly before Jesus was crucified, He visited good friends in a small town outside Jerusalem. It was here that Mary would anoint Jesus' feet after He had raised Lazarus, her brother, from the dead. As Lazarus came out of the tomb, Jesus told everyone to help remove the graveclothes that were wrapped around him. Even as he responded in obedience to Jesus' powerful command, coming out of the darkness and into the light, Lazarus still needed the help of other people to take off what had formerly bound him in death (see John 11:1-44).

The Lord spent His final days in the company of friends. Meals were shared. Gifts were given. Love was expressed. Truth was spoken. You can only imagine the thoughts and feelings swirling in the hearts and minds of the people who took hold of Lazarus's graveclothes or who sat at the table to break bread with Jesus.

With this picture of new life in mind, read the following passage.

<blockquote>
Taste and see that the LORD is good.
How happy is the person who takes refuge in him!
You who are his holy ones, fear the LORD,
for those who fear him lack nothing.
Young lions lack food and go hungry,
but those who seek the LORD
will not lack any good thing.
Come, children, listen to me;
I will teach you the fear of the LORD.
Who is someone who desires life,
loving a long life to enjoy what is good?
Keep your tongue from evil
and your lips from deceitful speech.
Turn away from evil and do what is good;
seek peace and pursue it.
PSALM 34:8-14
</blockquote>

Read Psalm 34 in your Bible. Let it guide a time of prayerful reflection.

WALKING IN THE SPIRIT

Start

———

We'll start by reviewing what we learned in the previous week's personal studies. Refer to your notes in week 6, especially day 5, when answering these questions with the group.

What new truth did you learn, or what stood out to you this week?

What details in your life had you previously failed to recognize as part of your worship (day 1)?

What are some ways we justify holding on to parts of the old self instead of removing and discarding them (day 2)?

How have you noticed yourself speaking, thinking, or acting in a way that shows a lack of full trust in God?

Jesus' redemptive work makes a new identity possible, and we must lean on the Holy Spirit to know how to move forward in this identity. However, we must remain aware that the enemy seeks to disrupt and discredit the identity and inheritance we have in Christ.

After praying, watch the video teaching.

Watch

Use this section to take notes as you watch video session 7.

The Holy Spirit is God inhabiting us.

How to Walk in the Spirit

1. Be saved.

2. Be baptized.

3. Be repentant.

4. Be filled with the Spirit.

5. Believe the Word.

6. Be prayerful.

7. Be obedient.

The Holy Spirit will empower us to do what we can't do on our own.

The Holy Spirit is never going to lead us to do anything contrary to the Word of God.

Discuss

After viewing the video, discuss the following questions with your group.

How do you feel or what do you think when you hear about following or listening to the Holy Spirit? Why do you think we have so many different reactions to or ideas about the Holy Spirit?

According to the Scriptures shared in the video, what does the Holy Spirit do? What does He enable you to do?

Read Ephesians 6:10-20. Whose strength do you stand in? How does this mental picture reveal the partnership between God's work and our work?

How do you feel or what do you think when you hear a reference to the devil and spiritual warfare? Why do you think we have so many different reactions to or ideas about Satan and spiritual warfare?

Why is it vital to our lives in Christ for us to live with an awareness of the Holy Spirit's role and of Satan's attacks?

What happens if we live as if spiritual warfare isn't real?

Read Ephesians 5:15-17. What could you do this week to be more careful and wise about making the most of each opportunity to do God's will each day?

In what ways has this session been encouraging, convicting, or well timed?

After discussion, close the session with prayer.

Day 1
FILLED WITH THE SPIRIT

To walk by the Holy Spirit, you must be filled with the Holy Spirit. To be filled with the Holy Spirit, you must be in a redemptive relationship with Jesus Christ. At the moment you believed the gospel, you received a deposit on your salvation in the form of God, the Holy Spirit (see 2 Cor. 1:21-22; Eph. 1:13-14). The Spirit fills us with His presence and begins to work in our lives to make us more like Jesus. Paul contrasted being full of the Spirit with being full of wine:

> *Don't get drunk with wine, which leads*
> *to reckless living, but be filled by the Spirit.*
> **EPHESIANS 5:18**

When people are drunk, they aren't completely aware of their surroundings, words, and actions. They lose coordination and may even bring harm to themselves or others. In contrast, being filled by the Spirit means you have greater control of yourself, especially your words and actions, and a heightened awareness of your surroundings. You're fully available to be used by God in the moment—completely focused on His desires instead of your own. Your heart, body, and mind are in tune with His activity, moving with Him in a way that brings life and healing to others.

Read Romans 8:1-6. What benefits do we receive when the Holy Spirit takes up residence in our hearts?

The Holy Spirit empowers you to embrace God's will in your life. He testifies that you aren't condemned and consigned to death but alive and able to live out God's will and purpose for your life. The filling of the Holy Spirit allows us to set our minds on the priorities and purposes of God.

At the end of His earthly ministry, on the night before Jesus was betrayed and then crucified, He taught His disciples at length about the Holy Spirit. Many of Christ's more explicit teachings about the Spirit are found in John 14–16.

Identify the names and purposes of the Holy Spirit in the following passages.

John 14:15-17

John 14:26

John 15:26

John 16:7-11

John 16:13-15

Based on these teachings of Jesus, what's the primary role of the Holy Spirit?

A few other themes dominate these chapters describing the roles of the Holy Spirit. Previous weeks of study have touched on these themes, such as the Spirit's intercession for you in prayer (see Rom. 8:26-27) and the Spirit's role in rooting you in Christ so that you can grow spiritually in His strength (see Eph. 3:16-21). Simply put, the Holy Spirit is Christ with you and in you.

Read the following verses and choose a word or a phrase to summarize each theme.

John 14:1,27; 16:33

John 14:13-14; 15:7,16; 16:23-24

John 14:12,15,21-23, 15:4,17

John 14:28; 15:11; 16:20-22

Thank the Holy Spirit for His presence and power in you. Pray that He will work in you and through you so that you can know and make known the life-changing truth of Jesus.

Day 2
SUFFER AS A SON

Walking with Christ isn't always an easy path. In fact, Jesus promised again and again that it would be difficult (especially see John 15:18–16:4). But His way is filled with grace even in suffering. You have a real enemy who opposes the image of God in you—the same enemy who was hissing poisonous lies in the garden—but you also have the Holy Spirit, who lives inside you to ensure ultimate victory:

> ¹⁶*The Spirit himself testifies together with our spirit that we are God's children, ¹⁷and if children, also heirs—heirs of God and coheirs with Christ—if indeed we suffer with him so that we may also be glorified with him.*
> ROMANS 8:16-17

According to verse 17, what two experiences will accompany your inheritance?

Paul offered two seemingly contradictory promises in these verse: you will suffer, and you will be glorified. These may be difficult to reconcile in your mind. But the Scriptures unite them. Jesus is God's perfect Son, but His sonship is clearly seen through what He suffered. In God's economy, suffering is evidence of sonship. John wrote about suffering as sons of God:

> *See what great love the Father has given us that we should be called God's children—and we are! The reason the world does not know us is that it didn't know him.*
> 1 JOHN 3:1

> *Everyone who believes that Jesus is the Christ has been born of God, and everyone who loves the Father also loves the one born of him. This is how we know that we love God's children: when we love God and obey his commands. For this is what love for God is: to keep his commands. And his commands are not a burden, because everyone who has been born of God conquers the world. This is the victory that has conquered the world: our faith.*
> 1 JOHN 5:1-4

Reading the Book of 1 John is like attending a seminar on how to apply Jesus' teachings from John 14–16 to your daily life.

In the midst of struggle, suffering, and spiritual attack, what's the battle plan, according to 1 John?

In Ephesians Paul provided a blueprint for navigating suffering and spiritual battles:

> *Be strengthened by the Lord and by his vast strength. Put on the full armor of God so that you can stand against the schemes of the devil. For our struggle is not against flesh and blood, but against the rulers, against the authorities, against the cosmic powers of this darkness, against evil, spiritual forces in the heavens. For this reason take up the full armor of God, so that you may be able to resist in the evil day, and having prepared everything, to take your stand.*
> EPHESIANS 6:10-13

What reminder did Paul provide about opposition to your faith? Why is this reality so important to keep in mind?

What three actions does Paul instruct you to take in your suffering?

1.
2.
3.

Over the next few days you'll take a close look at the armor of God and instructions for standing firm against the devil and his attacks. Don't be surprised that he hates you and that the world hates you. Spiritual opposition is part of being in the family of God. But don't be caught unprepared either, taking lightly the schemes of the devil. Pray now for vigilance and perseverance:

> *Be of sober spirit, be on the alert. Your adversary, the devil, prowls around like a roaring lion, seeking someone to devour.*
> 1 PETER 5:8, NASB

Day 3
SEEK TRUTH

Stand, therefore, with truth like a belt around your waist, righteousness like armor on your chest, and your feet sandaled with readiness for the gospel of peace. In every situation take up the shield of faith with which you can extinguish all the flaming arrows of the evil one. Take the helmet of salvation and the sword of the Spirit—which is the word of God.
EPHESIANS 6:14-17

What's the purpose of a belt as a piece of armor? Why would it be important to secure this piece of armor first when preparing for spiritual warfare?

How does truth relate to rightly putting on and handling the other armor?

In the account of David's preparation for battle against Goliath, the giant and the enemy of God's people, King Saul dressed the young shepherd boy in his armor. The scene in Scripture is almost comical as David tried to walk in the borrowed armor of the tall leader. Imagine a young child dressing in his or her parent's clothes. David knew the armor didn't fit properly and was therefore untrustworthy. Instead, like Paul, he boldly proclaimed that he knew the One he trusted. The truth of God had been proved to him; this bulky armor hadn't.

Without God's truth you're left to clumsily and perhaps dangerously moving out in your own opinions about the way of righteousness, the gospel, salvation, and Scripture. When you're wrapped tightly in the truth, however, you can move freely and confidently, knowing the other pieces of armor securely fit in their proper place.

We find truth as we seek wisdom that comes only from God:

Trust in the LORD with all your heart
And do not lean on your own understanding.
In all your ways acknowledge Him,
And He will make your paths straight.
PROVERBS 3:5-6, NASB

Our culture has taught us that truth is found inside ourselves. Scripture teaches that truth is found in the Lord. When are you most tempted to follow your own understanding?

When has following your own understanding led to grief and pain? When has listening to the Lord led to life and purpose?

God's truth is meant to lead us to abundant joy and eternal satisfaction (see Ps. 16:11). The best the world's wisdom can offer us is fleeting pleasure. Truth is found when we look to God and His truth for our direction, resisting the allure of the world's wisdom, resting in the promise that the Spirit will guide us into truth (see John 16:13), and remembering that God's truth may seem foolish to a fallen world.

Read 1 Corinthians 1:18-31. How did Paul contrast worldly wisdom with the wisdom of the cross?

What do these verses teach you about the nature of God's truth?

How will you commit to seek God's truth instead of seeking the wisdom of the world?

We find God's truth in God's Word, which we will consider in tomorrow's study. The Holy Spirit uses God's Word to shape God's people with God's truth. Conclude your study by thanking God for putting the desire for truth in your heart. Commit to seek Him daily and intentionally so that you can declare His praises.

Day 4
GET INTO THE WORD

To hear the Holy Spirit, you have to read the Word He inspired. How else or where else would you go to seek truth? Read what Paul wrote as he mentored Timothy:

> *All Scripture is inspired by God and is profitable for teaching, for*
> *rebuking, for correcting, for training in righteousness, so that the*
> *man of God may be complete, equipped for every good work.*
> 2 TIMOTHY 3:16-17

The word translated here as "inspired" literally means "God-breathed." What does this phrase reveal about the nature of "all Scripture" (v. 16)?

What four functions is Scripture profitable for? How would you define each?

Highlight the words "complete, equipped for every good work" (v. 17). How does Paul's conclusion about the benefit of Scripture relate to your identity as God's workmanship (see Eph. 2:10)?

When Paul wrote this second letter to Timothy, he had already written him before about "training in righteousness" (2 Tim. 3:16). In his first letter Paul had contrasted this training to wasting time with "silly myths" (1 Tim. 4:7). In other words, seeking the truth is a matter of personal training:

> *Have nothing to do with pointless and silly myths. Rather, train yourself*
> *in godliness. For the training of the body has limited benefit, but godliness*
> *is beneficial in every way, since it holds promise for the present life and also*
> *for the life to come. This saying is trustworthy and deserves full acceptance.*
> *For this reason we labor and strive, because we have put our hope in the*
> *living God, who is the Savior of all people, especially of those who believe.*
> 1 TIMOTHY 4:7-10

How do words like *training, labor,* and *strive* help you understand your responsibility in seeking truth and growing in godliness?

Be diligent to present yourself approved to God as a workman who does not need to be ashamed, accurately handling the word of truth.
2 TIMOTHY 2:15, NASB

"Accurately handling the word of truth" takes practice, familiarity, and wisdom. It's dangerous to use Scripture in a way it wasn't intended to be used. People can get hurt. Throwing Bible verses around carelessly and out of context is as reckless as Peter's action when he grabbed a sword and tried to defend Jesus on the night of His arrest, cutting of a man's ear. The Bible is a sword but one to be wielded responsibly:

Take the helmet of salvation and the sword of the Spirit—which is the word of God.
EPHESIANS 6:17

The "sword of the Spirit—which is the word of God" is the only weapon in Paul's list of armor. As you prepare for spiritual warfare, temptation, suffering, and all kinds of attack, rightly handling Scripture is your best defense and offense.

Read Matthew 4:1-11. Notice the back-and-forth of spiritual warfare. What can you learn from Jesus' example in battling temptation and attack?

The scene is a verbal duel, each opponent wielding a sword. Unlike Adam and Eve, who quoted God's command but then fell for the serpent's lie, Jesus rightly handled the truth, quoting Scripture and standing firm against the attacks. Satan tried to misuse Scripture, pulling it out of context and twisting the truth into lies. But Jesus defeated His enemy, not by displaying miraculous power but by rightly handling God's Word.

Conclude your time of study by asking the Holy Spirit to give you a hunger for God's Word:

It is written: "Man must not live on bread alone but on every word that comes from the mouth of God."
MATTHEW 4:4

Day 5
TAKE FIVE: SPIRIT

Use the space below to record five main takeaways God taught you through the group session and personal studies this week. You may want to choose one truth from each day, or certain days may have been especially meaningful to you.

1.

2.

3.

4.

5.

One of the most incredible accounts of personal faith and the power of the Holy Spirit is the example of the young virgin girl named Mary (see Luke 1:26-38). An angel appeared to her, revealing God's plan for her life and for the world. Even though it was biologically impossible, Mary believed she would become pregnant and give birth to the Son of God. Her husband, Joseph, was also visited by the angel, who revealed the good news and instructed him not to divorce Mary and not to be intimate with her until after Jesus' birth (see Matt. 1:18-25). Only the miraculous power of the Holy Spirit could explain the blessing God chose to entrust to Mary and Joseph. Mary's response was full of obedient faith:

> *"I am the Lord's servant," said Mary. "May*
> *it be done to me according to your word."*
> LUKE 1:38

As you ponder Mary's response of faith, read the following passage.

> *How happy are those whose way is blameless,*
> *who walk according to the LORD's instruction!*
> *Happy are those who keep his decrees*
> *and seek him with all their heart.*
> *They do nothing wrong;*
> *they walk in his ways.*
> *How can a young man keep his way pure?*
> *By keeping your word.*
> *I have sought you with all my heart;*
> *don't let me wander from your commands.*
> *I have treasured your word in my heart*
> *so that I may not sin against you.*
> PSALM 119:1-3,9-11

Read Psalm 119:1-16 in your Bible. Let it guide a time of prayerful reflection.

Week 8

WALKING
ON MISSION

Discuss

After viewing the video, discuss the following questions with your group.

What points in the video were most significant for you?

How has this Bible study defined work in general? How has it defined our purpose in Christ?

Read Matthew 22:37-40. What have you learned about each of the following jobs the Lord has given to you?
• Love God with all you are.
• Love other people as yourself.
• Share with people the good news of salvation in Christ.
• Help people become mature followers of Jesus.

What are some ways God has uniquely created you for the work He has prepared for you to do?
• What gifts do people see in you?
• What passions and abilities do you have?
• What burdens and experiences do you have?

How could you serve others in your church for the sake of God's mission? Help one another identify needs and ways you can meet those needs as individuals and as a group.

What would you tell somebody who asked what you learned in this study? How have your perspective and life changed from studying God's Word?

After discussion, close the session with prayer.

Day 1
GIFTS

The LORD God said, "It is not good for the man to be alone.
I will make a helper corresponding to him."
GENESIS 2:18

From the very beginning God created us for relationships. After repeatedly declaring His creation good and before sin entered the world, God described something as "not good." It wasn't because the man was lacking. He was created in the image of God, in personal fellowship with God, in a paradise setting. Obviously, there are practical reasons a male and a female are both needed to be fruitful and multiply according to God's design, but this statement has more profound implications than biology.

How did God describe His intended design for this first human relationship?

Every person has unique talents and abilities that make him or her a valuable contributor to God's work in the world. God could have created the world to work any way He wanted, but He chose to fill it with a diversity of personalities, abilities, and gifts. In addition, He designed the diversity to fit together in a glorious unity, weaving a tapestry of His grace and goodness.

In the final week of this Bible study, you'll look closely at the nature of these interwoven human relationships and the work with which God has blessed you. Today we'll focus on the way He has uniquely wired you. Last week you were introduced to the work of the Holy Spirit in your life. Another function of the Spirit is to bestow divinely selected gifts on every believer in Christ:

There are different gifts, but the same Spirit. There are different
ministries, but the same Lord. And there are different activities,
but the same God produces each gift in each person. A manifestation
of the Spirit is given to each person for the common good:
1 CORINTHIANS 12:4-7

What did Paul say about the purpose of spiritual gifts? How is this purpose consistent with the purpose of human relationships as revealed in the creation story?

Read 1 Corinthians 12:8-11. What's the repeated emphasis in this list of gifts?

Read 1 Corinthians 12:12-31. What does this passage reveal about the diversity of gifts?

The following chapter in Paul's letter to the church in Corinth is a popular one. It's often read at weddings. For many people, it's inspiring poetry. What tends to be forgotten is that the love chapter, as it's sometimes called, comes in the middle of Paul's teaching on spiritual gifts. It begins:

> *If I speak human or angelic tongues but do not have love, I am a noisy gong or a clanging cymbal. If I have the gift of prophecy and understand all mysteries and all knowledge, and if I have all faith so that I can move mountains but do not have love, I am nothing. And if I give away all my possessions, and if I give over my body in order to boast but do not have love, I gain nothing.*
> 1 CORINTHIANS 13:1-3

Read 1 Corinthians 13:8-13. After the gifts have served their purpose, what three things will remain? What does their enduring quality teach you about their desirability?

Ask the Holy Spirit to show you how He has uniquely gifted you for the sake of the common good among God's people. Consider ways you can serve the local church. Pray that most of all, the Spirit will bless you with faith, hope, and love—the greatest gifts.

Day 2
THE CHURCH

Have you ever believed the common misconception that spirituality is a private matter and that therefore you can believe in Jesus without belonging to a church? Although it's true that faith is a personal relationship with God, you'd be wasting your time to find examples of Christians in the New Testament who weren't in relationships with other believers. It's not that they felt obligated to join a church; they wanted to. In their new identities in Christ, they desired community. As children of the Heavenly Father, they became brothers and sisters in Christ. So while Christian faith is personal, it's not private. It's actually quite public and intrinsically communal:

> *As it is, there are many parts, but one body. The eye cannot say to the hand, "I don't need you!" Or again, the head can't say to the feet, "I don't need you!"*
> 1 CORINTHIANS 12:20-21

What was Paul's point in using the image of the body and its parts? What did the body represent? What did the parts represent?

Paul also used this image in his letter to the Ephesians, calling believers to live out our identity and purpose in relationship with the church.

Read Ephesians 4:11-13. What's the purpose of leadership roles in the church?

Read Ephesians 4:14-16. What's the purpose of serving the church?

The letter goes on to describe the new life and purpose of members of Christ's body. Reminding the Ephesian believers of their radical transformation from darkness into light, Paul called them to "pay careful attention, then, to how you live—

not as unwise people but as wise—making the most of the time, because the days are evil" (Eph. 5:15-16). What did he mean? Christians go into the world—together as ambassadors—to call people out of a dark, evil world and into light:

> *We are ambassadors for Christ, since God is making his appeal*
> *through us. We plead on Christ's behalf: "Be reconciled to God."*
> *He made the one who did not know sin to be sin for us,*
> *so that in him we might become the righteousness of God.*
> 2 CORINTHIANS 5:20-21

The church is on mission to call people out of darkness and into light. The best thing we can do for other people is to tell them how they can find their purpose in Christ. You're part of the body of Christ. You've been filled with His Spirit for His purpose. You're His ambassador, representing His authority and proclaiming the good news of the gospel throughout the world. He's making all things new (see Rev. 21:5). Beyond the warfare there's victory.

The next time you're tempted to think you don't need the church, don't like the church, or don't even want go to church, remind yourself that you're the church. You're part of the church. It's who you are. You need the church, and the church needs you. Why? For the sake of God's work. And you have only a season before time is up and He makes all things new. The writer of Hebrews admonishes:

> *Let us watch out for one another to provoke love and good works,*
> *not neglecting to gather together, as some are in the habit of doing, but*
> *encouraging each other, and all the more as you see the day approaching.*
> HEBREWS 10:24-25

Where will you commit to serving and belonging at your church?

Pray now for your local church. If you aren't yet a member of one, pray that God will guide you to a healthy church. Thank Him that even though no church community is perfect because it's made of broken parts, it's still His plan for blessing you and the world. Pray that you'll make the most of every opportunity to help others grow to maturity in Christ and that you'll take seriously your responsibility as Christ's ambassador, boldly proclaiming His praise and pleading with others to be born again through faith in the gospel and receive a new identity in Him.

Day 3
ON MISSION TO THE WORLD

Pray at all times in the Spirit with every prayer and request, and stay alert with all perseverance and intercession for all the saints. Pray also for me, that the message may be given to me when I open my mouth to make known with boldness the mystery of the gospel. For this I am an ambassador in chains. Pray that I might be bold enough to speak about it as I should.
EPHESIANS 6:18-20

How did Paul refer to himself? What was his current situation?

What did Paul ask for? What does his request tell you about God's mission?

As Paul concluded his letter to the churches around Ephesus, he made it clear that nothing could stop God's work in and through His people—His mission to the world. Paul was in prison, yet he saw even his imprisonment as an opportunity to be on mission instead of a hopeless situation.

The Book of Acts is the record of the birth and growth of the church. Some scholars have suggested that it could be called the Acts of the Holy Spirit because the Spirit was the One at work in and through God's people to spread the gospel. The Book opens with a scene in which Jesus and His disciples were together one last time:

> *When they had come together, they asked him, "Lord, are you restoring the kingdom to Israel at this time?" He said to them, "It is not for you to know times or periods that the Father has set by his own authority. But you will receive power when the Holy Spirit has come on you, and you will be my witnesses in Jerusalem, in all Judea and Samaria, and to the end of the earth."*
> ACTS 1:6-8

What did Jesus tell them to do? What identity and purpose did He identify?

What did Jesus promise them? Why was this promise essential to their identity and mission?

Matthew recorded similar instructions at the end of his Gospel. The Great Commission, as it's known, expresses the purpose of everyone who believes in Jesus. By His authority you're Christ's ambassador. You're His witness. You have a mission:

> *Jesus came near and said to them, "All authority has been given to me in heaven and on earth. Go, therefore, and make disciples of all nations, baptizing them in the name of the Father and of the Son and of the Holy Spirit, teaching them to observe everything I have commanded you. And remember, I am with you always, to the end of the age."*
> MATTHEW 28:18-20

What essential actions in disciple making do these verses identify?

Why is disciple making an essential component of faith for all followers of Jesus?

The word *disciple* is the core of your new identity in Christ. A disciple learns from a teacher to become like the teacher. The purpose of being witnesses isn't merely to spread information, awareness, or even awe. It's to make more worshipers of Jesus. It's to make disciples of all nations. It's to be fruitful and multiply, filling the earth with the image of God.

Jesus is the Alpha and Omega. You know how the story began in Genesis and how it ends in Revelation. Join the multitudes now in praising your King—the One who died and rose again, with all authority in heaven and on earth (see Rev. 7:9-10).

Day 4
REMEMBER WHO YOU ARE

Review the following verses and record a first-person summary of each. For example, John 3:16 would be "God loved me in this way: He gave his one and only Son, so that I would believe in him and not perish but have eternal life." Your summary doesn't have to be exact wording but should express and personally apply the key truth in each text.

Genesis 1:27-28

Genesis 3:8-9

God created you, came to you after you sinned, and called you out of darkness and shame. This is still true. Your identity comes with a responsibility. You were created for a purpose. God made you to reflect and replicate His image until the earth is full of His glory and praise. You've been born again through faith in the gospel of Jesus and sent out in His authority to make more disciples—children of His marvelous light—in every nation.

Continue recording first-person summaries of the following verses.

Ephesians 1:3-4

Ephesians 1:7-10

Ephesians 1:13-14

Ephesians 2:1-2

Ephesians 2:8-10

Ephesians 2:19

Ephesians 3:11

Ephesians 4:4-7

Ephesians 4:20-24

Ephesians 5:15-21

Ephesians 6:11-12

Ephesians 6:13-17

Ephesians 6:18-20

Conclude this time of review by reflecting on the glorious truths of your identity and purpose in Christ. Remember, who you are is defined by whose you are. Your Creator and King, your Savior and Lord, has called you by name. You are His. Go spread the good news.

Day 5
TAKE FIVE: PURPOSE

Use the space below to record five main takeaways God taught you through the group session and personal studies this week. You may want to choose one truth from each day, or certain days may have been especially meaningful to you.

1.

2.

3.

4.

5.

Do you know who were the first witnesses of the resurrection? In the final chapter of Matthew's Gospel, following the death and burial of Jesus and before the Great Commission, the account is recorded of an angel rolling the heavy stone away from the tomb and proclaiming the good news to Mary Magdelene and another Mary. The angel sent the women to tell the disciples about Jesus' resurrection. The description of what occurred next is astounding:

> *Departing quickly from the tomb with fear and great joy, they ran to tell his disciples the news. Just then Jesus met them and said, "Greetings!" They came up, took hold of his feet, and worshiped him. Then Jesus told them, "Do not be afraid. Go and tell my brothers to leave for Galilee, and they will see me there."*
> MATTHEW 28:8-10

Take hold of His feet now in personal worship. Knowing that experiencing Jesus should lead to spreading the good news, read the following passage.

> *Sing a new song to the LORD;*
> *let the whole earth sing to the LORD.*
> *Sing to the LORD, bless his name;*
> *proclaim his salvation from day to day.*
> *Declare his glory among the nations,*
> *his wondrous works among all peoples.*
> *Say among the nations: "The LORD reigns.*
> *The world is firmly established; it cannot be shaken.*
> *He judges the peoples fairly."*
> *Let the heavens be glad and the earth rejoice;*
> *let the sea and all that fills it resound.*
> *Let the fields and everything in them celebrate.*
> *Then all the trees of the forest will shout for joy*
> *before the LORD, for he is coming—*
> *for he is coming to judge the earth.*
> *He will judge the world with righteousness*
> *and the peoples with his faithfulness.*
> PSALM 96:1-3,10-13

Read Psalm 96 in your Bible. Let it guide a time of prayerful reflection.

TIPS FOR LEADING A SMALL GROUP

Prayerfully Prepare

Prepare for each group session with prayer. Ask the Holy Spirit to work through you and the group discussion as you point to Jesus each week through God's Word.

REVIEW the personal studies and the group sessions ahead of time.

PRAY for each person in the group.

Minimize Distractions

Do everything in your ability to help people focus on what's most important: connecting with God, with the Bible, and with one another.

Create a comfortable environment. If group members are uncomfortable, they'll be distracted and therefore not engaged in the group experience.

Take into consideration seating, temperature, lighting, refreshments, surrounding noise, and general cleanliness.

At best, thoughtfulness and hospitality show guests and group members they're welcome and valued in whatever environment you choose to gather. At worst, people may never notice your effort, but they're also not distracted.

Include Others

Your goal is to foster a community in which people are welcome just as they are but encouraged to grow spiritually. Always be aware of opportunities to include anyone who visits the group and invite new people to join your group.

Encourage Discussion

A good small-group experience has the following characteristics.

EVERYONE PARTICIPATES. Encourage everyone to ask questions, share responses, or read aloud.

NO ONE DOMINATES—NOT EVEN THE LEADER. Be sure your time speaking as a leader takes up less than half your time together as a group. Politely guide the discussion if anyone dominates.

NOBODY IS RUSHED THROUGH QUESTIONS. Don't feel that a moment of silence is a bad thing. People often need time to think about their responses to questions they've just heard or to gain courage to share what God is stirring in their hearts.

INPUT IS AFFIRMED AND FOLLOWED UP. Make sure you point out something true or helpful in a response. Don't just move on. Build community with follow-up questions, asking how other people have experienced similar things or how a truth has shaped their understanding of God and the Scripture you're studying. People are less likely to speak up if they fear that you don't actually want to hear their answers or that you're looking for only a certain answer.

GOD AND HIS WORD ARE CENTRAL. Opinions and experiences can be helpful, but God has given us the truth. Trust Scripture to be the authority and God's Spirit to work in people's lives. You can't change anyone, but God can. Continually point people to the Word and to active steps of faith.

Keep Connecting

Think of ways to connect with group members during the week. Participation during the group session always improves when members spend time connecting with one another outside the group sessions. The more people are comfortable with and involved in one another's lives, the more they'll look forward to being together. When people move beyond being friendly to truly being friends who form a community, they come to each session eager to engage instead of merely attending.

LEADER GUIDE

How to Use This Leader Guide

Prepare to Lead

Each session in the leader guide is designed to be cut out so that you, the leader, can keep this front-and-back page with you as you lead the group session.

Work through the personal studies, watch the session's teaching video, and read the group session with the leader guide cutout in hand to understand how it supplements each section of the group study.

The Big Picture

Use this section to help focus your preparation and leadership during the group session. Take note of the highlighted points.

Key Scriptures

Key passages of Scripture are listed for quick reference.

Considerations

The purpose of leading a group is to bring God's Word to the people in the group. This section is designed to help you consider and wrestle with the ideas in each session and to suggest ways to apply those truths to your group.

Pray

Use the prayer provided to close the group session.

SESSION 1

The Big Picture

This first session introduces foundational questions such as: What is identity? Why is it important? How do we define ourselves? Who has the authority to determine our identity? The answers to these questions are more practical—and less abstract—than we may realize.

In session 1 Stephen and Alex teach on the God who made us and what it means to be made in His image. Four key truths about God provide the foundation for our identities.

1. God created us, so He has the right to determine our identity.
2. God owns us and bought us with a price, so he has the double right.
3. God has all authority over all other authorities, so he has the triple right.
4. God knows us best, so He has four levels of authority.

Key Scriptures

Genesis 1:26-28
Psalm 24:1
Psalm 139:1-4,16
Isaiah 64:8
1 Corinthians 6:19-20

Considerations

Ultimately, you want to help group members say, "Yes, God made me. He created and chose me in His sovereignty in this way and for this time." The focus should be on the image of God, the *imago Dei,* because although all people are created in the image of God, not all people are redeemed by God (redemption will be introduced in session 3). Multiple passages refer to the value of people, based on their creation in the image of God (see Gen. 1–2). This is why murder is wrong (see Gen. 9:6) and why cursing people is wrong (see Jas. 3:9-10). You may want to highlight the words used in Psalm 139 to describe the way God values people: they are "remarkably and wondrously made" (v. 14). "Precious" are His thoughts toward them (v. 17).

Ask members, on a scale of 1 to 10, how valuable they think they really are. With what value do they treat the people around them? Do they curse them? Do they honor and respect them? Like David, have they thanked and praised God for the way He made them and other people? They should thank God for their nationality, gender, parents, and godly heritage. This could be a great exercise to end the session.

Pray

Pray for group members to grow confident and certain about their God-given identity. Remind everyone to complete the personal studies before the next group session.

Notes

_____

_____

_____

_____

_____

_____

DEFINED

LEADER GUIDE

SESSION 2

The Big Picture

We've all rebelled against God's design at every level. Our hearts are wicked and depraved (see Jer. 17: 9). We're all broken uniquely; the root cause of our sin is universal, but its manifestations are personal. Jesus said He came to sinners because the sick are the ones who need a physician (see Matt. 9:12). Jesus came to save sinners because God recognized that people have broken, sinful hearts.

In session 2 Stephen and Alex help group members understand that though we're all children of God, we're broken both as individuals and as a whole and therefore separated from Him through original sin.

How should we respond to the desperate reality of personal sinfulness?

1. We must repent of our sins and place our trust in Jesus Christ for salvation.
2. We must follow God's Word to stop sinning and enjoy God's abundant life.
3. We must stop being distracted by other people's sins and address our own sinful condition.

Key Scriptures

Exodus 20:1-17
Matthew 15:18-20
Galatians 5
Ephesians 2:1-3

Considerations

During the discussion after the video, help people come face-to-face with the Scriptures by asking questions that reveal their sinfulness and brokenness. Using the Ten Commandments, walk through an inventory of sinfulness, asking, for example, *How many lies do you think you've told in your lifetime?* Responses could initially be humorous, but at the end of the day, the Word of God and the law of God will silence the mouths of people and will show them that they desperately need salvation, forgiveness, and transformation.

As sinners, people judge others, justify themselves, and withhold worship. We remove God from the throne, giving Him our leftover time, talents, and resources but not the first part of our days, our income, and our hearts.

Using Ephesians 2:1-3 as a starting point, define *sin* and consider ways sin has affected every area of our lives. Close with the fact that all people are either lost or saved, preparing for the gospel to come in session 3.

Pray

Thank God for His mercy and grace despite your sinfulness. Pray that He will convict your hearts in order to set them free and will fill them with the love of Christ and the power of the Holy Spirit. Remind everyone to complete the personal studies before the next group session.

Notes

_____
_____
_____
_____
_____
_____

DEFINED

LEADER GUIDE

SESSION 3

The Big Picture

In session 3 Stephen and Alex trace the change that happens when God moves in our lives and we receive the gospel. Ephesians 2:1-5 establishes the certainty we can have as followers of Christ. They outline seven evidences of salvation.

1. God's commands? Obedience

2. Who is Jesus? God, the Son

3. Response to sin? Repentance

4. Rebellion? God's discipline

5. Other believers? Love

6. Spiritual power? God's Spirit

7. Trusting for salvation? Jesus alone

Key Scriptures

2 Corinthians 5:17
Galatians 2:20
Ephesians 2:1-10

Considerations

Help group members understand that the gospel completely changes our identity. The gospel brings life where there was only death. The gospel gives us a hope and a future. Through the gospel God sees us the same way He sees His Son, as one who has never sinned. Nothing transforms like the gospel.

You may want to prepare in advance a brief personal testimony of the way Christ has changed your life. The more stories people hear of life change, the more likely they are to believe that their own lives can be changed and to open up about their thoughts, feelings, and experiences.

Pray

Pray together, thanking God for transforming your lives through Christ. Remind everyone to complete the personal studies before the next group session.

Notes

_____

_____

_____

_____

_____

_____

_____

_____

_____

_____

DEFINED

LEADER GUIDE

SESSION 4

The Big Picture

In session 4 Stephen and Alex work through Ephesians 1–2, pointing out all of the indicatives that are true of us now that we're in Christ, with a particular focus on Ephesians 1:1-14.

1. I'm blessed with every spiritual blessing (see v. 3).
2. I'm chosen, accepted, and beloved (see v. 4).
3. I'm a child of God (see v. 5).
4. I'm redeemed and forgiven (see v. 7).
5. I'm sealed with the Holy Spirit (see v. 13).

Those five realities result in five transformations. While session 1 featured realities that are true of all people, session 4 focuses on realities that are true of people who are in Christ. Again, the way we see our identity isn't an abstract notion. It has practical, real-life implications in the ways we—

1. view God, ourselves, our past, and our future;
2. think, speak, act, treat others, and pray;
3. handle success, failure, and loss;
4. react to criticism and false accusations;
5. respond to temptation and sin.

Key Scriptures

Ephesians 1:1-14
Ephesians 2:12-22

Considerations

Group members will be immersed in the declaratives or indicatives of our identity in Christ. Beyond the many blessings of being adopted sons and daughters, we're also God's inheritance. The discussion needs to reflect a before-and-after understanding:

- Before I was lost. Now God's Word says I'm found.
- Before I was an enemy of God. Now I'm a friend.
- Before I was a stranger. Now I'm adopted as a beloved son.
- Before I was dead in my sin. Now I'm alive.

Introduce Scripture verses to show members these contrasts.

Another important truth in this session is that we're a dwelling place of God.

Pray

Pray that God will overwhelm each of you with a sense of awe for the life-changing realities of your new life, as described in Ephesians 1–2. Ask Him to continue strengthening your unity as a group. Remind everyone to complete the personal studies before the next group session.

Notes

_____

_____

_____

_____

_____

_____

SESSION 5

The Big Picture

In session 5 Stephen and Alex explain all we've received in Christ, using key words in Ephesians. They demonstrate ways the Christian identity is different from the one the world promotes. With our new identity comes a rich inheritance given in wisdom and understanding. The Holy Spirit is the guarantee of our inheritance and the greatest blessing of our inheritance.

- We have salvation and eternal life.
- We have a loving Heavenly Father.
- We have blessings.
- We have a spiritual family.
- We have the Holy Spirit.
- We have power.
- We have provision.
- We have purpose, meaning, and value.
- We have the Word of God.
- We have a home in heaven waiting for us.
- We have a sure hope.

Key Scriptures

Ephesians 1:13-23
Philippians 4:19
Revelation 21:1-7
Revelation 22:1-5

Considerations

If the big picture of session 5 feels almost overwhelming, that's intentional. You want group members to feel a sense of overwhelming awe at all they've received in Christ. It's one thing to say we've received a rich inheritance. It's another thing to feel that this list barely scratches the surface in describing our incalculable riches in Christ.

Pray

Pray that the Holy Spirit will fill you with hope in Christ, granting you spiritual eyes with an eternal perspective. Spend a few moments praising Him for His infinite goodness. Remind everyone to complete the personal studies before the next group session.

Notes

_____

_____

_____

_____

_____

_____

_____

_____

_____

_____

_____

SESSION 6

The Big Picture

In session 6 Stephen and Alex transition from the first half of Ephesians to the second half. The final three chapters of Ephesians highlight the way God changes our words, our thinking, our attitudes, our habits, and our relationships.

Now that we know what it means to have an identity in Christ, we need to examine the process by which our identity becomes a part of who we are. According to Ephesians 4–5, we put off the old self and put on the new.

- Put off the old self; put on the new self (see 4:22-24).
- Put off lying; put on the truth (see 4:25).
- Put off stealing; put on working and sharing (see 4:28).
- Put off unwholesome speech; put on edifying words (see 4:29).
- Put off bitterness, anger, and slander; put on kindness and forgiveness (see 4:31-32).
- Put off sexual immorality, greed, and filthy talk; put on thanksgiving (see 5:3-4).
- Put off foolishness; put on God's will (see 5:17).
- Put off drunkenness; put on the filling of God's Spirit (see 5:18).
- Put on worship, thanksgiving, and submission to one another (see 5:19-21).

Key Scriptures

Ephesians 4:1-6,17-32
Ephesians 5:1-21

Considerations

Our new identity in Christ will be lived out in every area of our lives. Ask group members to make a before-and-after comparison in these areas:

- Marriage
- Parenting
- Work environment
- Words
- Thinking
- Attitudes
- Habits

Pray

Pray for one another. Consider dividing into pairs for an extended time of prayer, confession, and encouragement about living worthy of our calling in Christ. Ask God to remind everyone of the true joy and freedom found in faithfully obeying Christ rather than in following our hearts. Remind everyone to complete the personal studies before the next group session.

Notes

_____

_____

_____

_____

_____

_____

_____

DEFINED

LEADER GUIDE

SESSION 7

The Big Picture

The work of Jesus makes a new identity possible. We must lean on the Holy Spirit to learn how to move forward in this identity. We must remain aware, however, that an enemy seeks to disrupt and discredit the identity and inheritance we have in Christ.

In session 7 Stephen and Alex teach what it means to walk with the Spirit and to allow Him to lead us and give us direction. What exactly does the Holy Spirit do?

- The Holy Spirit saves.
- The Holy Spirit satisfies.
- The Holy Spirit helps us.
- The Holy Spirit teaches.
- The Holy Spirit convicts.
- The Holy Spirit guides.

Key Scriptures

Ephesians 5:15-21
Ephesians 6:10-20

Considerations

The Holy Spirit is often incredibly intriguing or intimidating for people. For many members of your group, perhaps even for you, the Holy Spirit may be a subject you're less familiar with. As with the other topics in this study, the goal is to help people recognize that the reality of the Spirit as revealed in Scripture isn't an abstract idea or a mere theological belief. The Holy Spirit isn't an idea or a thing. He's the third Person of the Trinity—God the Father, Son, and Spirit.

Help group members prepare for the final two sessions of this study by clarifying that all of the truths you've studied and discussed in the first six sessions are mere head knowledge if the Holy Spirit doesn't work in and through us, instructing and empowering us to believe and behave in a way that honors Christ. Remind them that our culture believes what we do defines who we are. A biblical picture of identity is very different. In Christ, by the work of the Holy Spirit, what we do flows from who we are. Identity shapes everything about our lives.

Pray

Pray for discernment and perseverance. Ask the Holy Spirit to equip and empower each group member to withstand spiritual attacks and to live victoriously in Christ. Remind everyone to complete the personal studies before the next group session.

Notes

_____

_____

_____

_____

_____

_____

_____

DEFINED

SESSION 8

The Big Picture

In session 7 you discussed the amazing creations God has made us to be. In this final session Stephen and Alex discuss the amazing works God saves and enables us to do. Because we're God's workmanship, we can go on mission with God. This mission includes serving the church and the world around us.

Our identity enables us to do things we couldn't do before. As followers of Jesus, we're called to do the following.

- Love God with all we are.
- Love other people as ourselves.
- Share the best news in the world with people.
- Help people become mature followers of Jesus.

The best news is that as followers of Jesus, just as we couldn't save ourselves, we don't do new works by ourselves either. He helps us accomplish the work He has given us to do in the following ways.

- He gives us spiritual gifts.
- He gives us unique passions and skills.
- He gives us unique burdens and experiences.

Key Scriptures

Matthew 22:37-40
Ephesians 2:10
1 Peter 2:9-10

Considerations

We're God's workmanship to do good works. Each of us needs to serve the needs of our local church. Spend a few minutes thinking about the needs in your church and community. How could you and the members of your group serve together?

Consider in advance the people you know who may need to hear about the life-changing truths you've learned about life in Christ. Encourage group members to share what they've learned with others and to invite new people to join the group for your next study.

Be sure to leave plenty of time for review. Summarizing the truths that have been most meaningful and transformative will help members realize the long-term impact of this study. If there isn't enough time for a thoughtful review, consider scheduling a follow-up group session to review session 8's personal studies and to discuss everyone's thoughts and experiences.

Pray

Pray that the Holy Spirit will fill you so that you can accomplish the work God has prepared for you. Praise God for uniquely creating you as His workmanship. Thank Jesus for redeeming you and for entrusting you with gifts for serving others. Pray that you'll be good stewards of those gifts and of His gospel. Pray that He will continue to work in and through you.

Remind everyone to complete the personal studies to conclude this Bible study. This week's lessons will help you learn to walk in the Spirit and will provide a lens through which you can see God's purpose for your lives.

Notes

FROM THE CREATORS OF WAR ROOM

OVERCOMER

Inspired by the Kendrick brothers' new movie *OVERCOMER* (in theaters August 23) and written by the #1 *New York Times* best-selling author team behind *The Love Dare* and *The Battle Plan for Prayer*, comes an exciting new resource about discovering your God-given identity and embracing the wonder of who you were created to be.

Based on powerful insights from the scriptural book of Ephesians and seasoned with personal stories and practical wisdom, *Defined* challenges readers to let the One who knows you best be the One who guides your heart the most. It's time for all of us to live in the amazing light of His acceptance, abundance, and strength.

Learn more at LifeWay.com/OvercomerResources

PUBLISHING

LifeWay

AFFIRM Films A Sony Company © 2019 Columbia TriStar Marketing Group, Inc. All Rights Reserved.

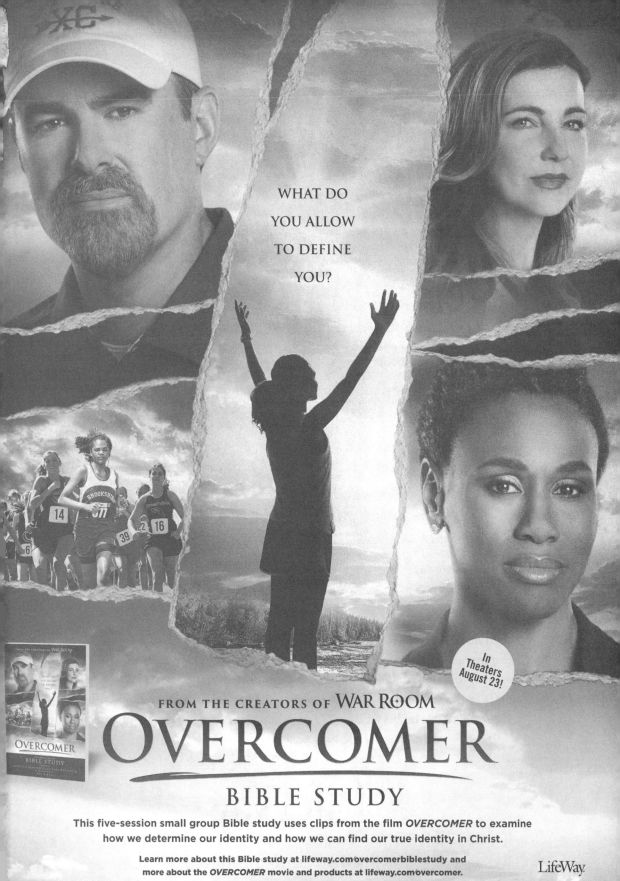

WHAT DO YOU ALLOW TO DEFINE YOU?

In Theaters August 23!

FROM THE CREATORS OF WAR ROOM

OVERCOMER

BIBLE STUDY

This five-session small group Bible study uses clips from the film *OVERCOMER* to examine how we determine our identity and how we can find our true identity in Christ.

Learn more about this Bible study at lifeway.com/overcomerbiblestudy and more about the *OVERCOMER* movie and products at lifeway.com/overcomer.

LifeWay

AFFIRM Films A Sony Company © 2019 Columbia TriStar Marketing Group, Inc. All Rights Reserved.

STUDY
WITH
THE
WHOLE
FAMILY

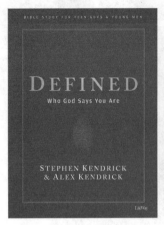

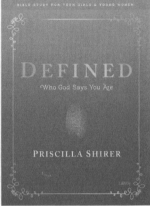

Guys Bible Study Book
$13.99 005815893

Guys Leader Kit
$59.99 005815899

Girls Bible Study Book
$13.99 005815892

Girls Leader Kit
$59.99 005815895

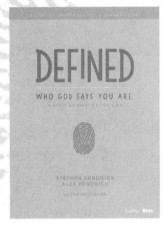

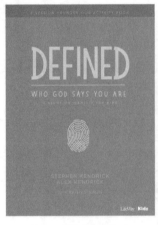

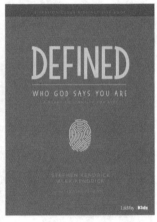

Kids Leader Guide
005814776 $14.99

Younger Kids Activity Book
005814773 $6.99

Older Kids Activity Book
005814775 $6.99

"Who am I?" Someone or something is attempting to answer the question for us. But to accurately answer this question, we must first ask, "Who does God say I am?" The Bible tells us that we are each made in God's image, but that image has become distorted by sin. The only way to restore what was broken is through a relationship with Jesus. These eight-session Bible studies for teen girls, guys, and kids examine spiritual truths found in the Book of Ephesians to address the topic of identity.

lifeway.com/defined